Bloodline for the Messiah

Bloodline for the Messiah

A. M. Deigloriam

RESOURCE *Publications* • Eugene, Oregon

BLOODLINE FOR THE MESSIAH

Copyright © 2019 A. M. Deigloriam. All rights reserved. Except for brief quotations in critical publications or reviews, no part of this book may be reproduced in any manner without prior written permission from the publisher. Write: Permissions, Wipf and Stock Publishers, 199 W. 8th Ave., Suite 3, Eugene, OR 97401.

Resource Publications
An Imprint of Wipf and Stock Publishers
199 W. 8th Ave., Suite 3
Eugene, OR 97401

www.wipfandstock.com

PAPERBACK ISBN: 978-1-5326-9519-3
HARDCOVER ISBN: 978-1-5326-9520-9
EBOOK ISBN: 978-1-5326-9521-6

Manufactured in the U.S.A. AUGUST 16, 2019

References throughout the book are from the King James translation of the Holy Bible.

Dedicated to my loving wife of 47 years, my family, and my many friends.

Contents

Background | ix
Introduction | xv

Creation | 1
Noah's ark and the flood | 4
Abraham and the Covenant | 8
Isaac and Rebekah | 15
Jacob the Leah | 18
Judah and Tamar | 22
Perez and wife unknown | 27
Hezron and wife unknown | 29
Ram and wife unknown | 32
Amminadab and wife unknown | 43
Nahshon and wife unknown | 49
Salmon and Rachab | 52
Boaz and Ruth | 55
Obed and wife unknown | 57
Jesse and wife unknown | 61
David and Bathsheba | 66
Solomon and Naamah | 72
Rehoboam and Maacah | 78
Abijah and wife unknown | 82
Asa and Azubah | 85
Jehoshaphat and wife unknown | 88
Jehoram and Athaliah | 93

The Gospel of Matthew | 97
Uzziah and Jerusha | 98
Jotham and Ahio | 101
Ahaz and Abijah | 103
Hezekiah and Hephzibah | 105
Manasseh and Meshullemeth | 109
Amon and Jedidah | 112
Josiah and Hamutal | 115
Babylonian Exile | 117
Jechoniah and wife unknown | 118
Salathiel and wife unknown | 121
Zerubbabel and Esthra | 123
Abiud and Tamita | 126
Azor and wife unknown | 130
Sadoc and Kaltimi | 132
Achim and Asbaoda | 134
Eliud and wife unknown | 136
Eleazar and Salome | 138
Matthan and Hazibah | 140
Jacob and Gadat | 142
Joseph and Mary | 144
Analysis | 148
Conclusion | 170

Bibliography | 183

Background

We live in a society that has rejected the idea of any type of moral standards and is focused entirely on protecting and recognizing the rights of all groups and religions regardless of their beliefs. In essence, governments are generally committed to enforcing their laws and do not care about the moral character of their citizens. This has resulted in a society that is keenly aware of laws and regulations and spends a great deal of money in trying to work around or avoid these laws. The idea of moral or ethical standards is never a consideration and in some cases may be viewed with some hostility. Unfortunately, the citizens that live under these conditions will need to comply with the practices of these societies in order to survive. We need to remember all the Christians that were martyred because they refused to worship the gods of Rome, Egypt and other countries.

Furthermore, many of the highly educated and accomplished in today's society do not believe in any type of religion and will take every opportunity to ridicule those that are believers. In addition, many of these highly successful individuals hold positions of responsibility where they can have an impact on young and impressionable minds. Again, moral values are not a consideration for many of these individuals and society will continue to deteriorate to a point where laws and regulations will be void of any religious foundation.

This situation has deteriorated to the point to where some pastors are now saying the Bible is not the inerrant word of God. These pastors are now editing and eliminating certain books of the Bible. Again, we have gone from scribes spending hundreds of years copying verses letter by letter to ensure there are no errors to pastors from major denominations now editing the Bible. Our Creator is a sovereign God who provided us with the Bible that we may have a path to follow. Matthew 5:18 reads, "For verily I say unto you, till heaven and earth pass, one jot or one tittle shall in no wise

Background

pass from the law, till all be fulfilled." God requires us to follow all of His laws in a spirit of righteousness. God is a personal loving God that deals with individuals on a one-on-one basis and only He can make a judgment. Pastors or other religious representatives cannot change God's laws to meet the wishes of individuals or organizations.

God's and man's view of success are contrary to each other. Jesus and His disciple were viewed as failures by the world. Wealth and status is not a measure of success in God's view. Success is recognizing your God-given talents and using them to the fullest to glorify God and show His love to others. Man has been given talents and the free will that allows man to use these talents as he wishes. A Christian that is successful will be using his talents to mature in Christ and be using their God-given talents to their fullest. Luke 12:48 reads, "For unto whomsoever much is given, of him shall be much required: and to whom men have committed much, of him they will ask the more." Joshua 1:8 reads, "This book of the law shall not depart out of thy mouth; but thou shalt meditate therein day and night, that thou mayest observe to do according to all that is written therein: for then thou shalt make thy way prosperous, and then thou shalt have good success."

The Bible consistently reminds us that the earth will pass away (Matt: 24:35) and only God's word will last forever. God created the earth from nothing and it will end in nothing. Man was created from nothing and will die with nothing. The only thing that will last from man will be his words and actions. Matthew 12:36 reads, "But I say unto you, That every idle word that men shall speak, they shall give account thereof in the day of judgment." Man's words and actions will determine his fate on judgment day. All sins are remembered and will be made known at judgment day for all of mankind. However, those who believed that God's only Son, Jesus Christ was born on this earth and died on the cross to forgive all sins will be given eternal life. John 3:16 reads, "For God so loved the world, that he gave his only begotten Son, that whosoever believeth in him should not perish, but have everlasting life."

Our understanding of God and His blessings is limited and in some cases simply wrong. He loves us and cares for us as we struggle between pride and its' desires and God's will and His desires for our lives. God's blessings are always connected to His purpose and for bringing us closer to Him. We have all gone through childhood, adolescence, adulthood, and in some cases parenthood and have gained some understanding how to use rewards and discipline in changing behavior. We generally stumble along and try desperately to match the right amount of reward and discipline to the right child in the right circumstance. In most cases with a lot of prayer and with God's grace our children manage to survive our many misguided and ineffective parenting skills. However, God knows us before we were born and knows our thoughts and words before they are spoken and is able to provide for us the right blessing and discipline for each situation.

Proverbs 6:16-19 reads, "These six things doth the Lord hate; yea, seven are an abomination unto Him: A proud look, a lying tongue, and hands that shed innocent blood, A heart that deviseth wicked imaginations, feet that be swift in running to mischief, A false witness that speaketh lies, and he that soweth discord among brethren."

We are vessels that are able to discern both good and evil. However, an increase in evil will result in a decrease in good in this vessel to the point where wickedness will eliminate all good. Evil will contaminate this vessel and destroy its witness unless forgiveness is prayed for with a contrite heart. Matthew 24:12 reads, "And because iniquity shall abound, the love of many shall wax cold." As we travel though this life we begin to realize and grow in appreciation of God's many blessings as we look back and see what God has done in our lives. It is important that we identify these many blessings and thank God for each blessing to allow His Spirit to strengthen and complete these blessings in our lives. We would not have survived many situations if it were not for God's loving hand that guided us or protected us from harm or evil. God will allow certain people into our lives that will warn us of pending danger. Again, it is important that we stop and recognize these words of concern and change direction. Thanking God for each of these blessings and praising His name is a life-long process for the obedient Christian. Psalm 100:4 reads, "Enter into his gates with thanksgiving, and into his courts with praise: be thankful unto him, and bless his name." God is our Creator and we are His people. We are His sheep in His pasture. We have done nothing that deserves this gift of life and our primary purpose in this life is to praise His name and share His love with others. There is no room for self or pride. The pride of man has infected many academics to believe there is no God, man has no soul, and life that we live is simply a biological process. In this vessel we live in we can consider both good and evil throughout our entire lives. As we grow closer to our Savior we encounter greater and more frequent attacks from Satan and his demons. We are in a war that requires us to put on the armor of God and His word.

Background

We have a fallen nature and live in a fallen world. The pagan gods of the past have been replaced today by the pagan god of money. The entire social structure of the world is based on money and the status and value society places on money. Violence continues to increase as more and more people are isolated and aliened by greed and inequitable systems. People will kill, steal, and lie to gain more money. Both the church and government need to reevaluate their priorities and take action to resolve the violence.

Faith is the element in our lives that confirms our soul to salvation. It was God's breath in the beginning that created man as a spiritual being with a soul. Since we were created by God we realize this separation and long for the reunion with our Creator. There is nothing on this earth that can fill that void. We were created for a life here on earth and in heaven. The soul will live for eternity and needs to be fed and nourished as a living being. Matthew 10:28 reads, "And fear not them which kill the body, but are not able to kill the soul; but rather fear him which is able to destroy both the soul and body in hell." Jesus spoke and healed many during His time on earth, but many still did not believe. Even though many witnessed these great miracles they refused to believe in Jesus as their Savior. In this case, seeing did not result in believing. John 5:37-38 reads, "And the Father himself, which hath sent me, hath borne witness of me. Ye have neither heard his voice at any time, nor seen his shape. And ye have not his word abiding in you: for whom he hath sent, him ye believe not." Peter was acting on faith as he stepped out of the boat and into the water. He was confident and knew without any doubt that Jesus was who He said He was. Peter's faith allowed him to act on his belief. Faith comes from hearing God's word and allowing God to control our lives and to continue in the process of dying to self. Faith in God will result in the love of His word and for the love of your neighbor. 1 Peter 1:7 reads, "That the trial of your faith, being much more precious than of gold that perisheth, though it be tried with fire, might be found unto praise and honor and glory at the appearing of Jesus Christ." The tested and refined faith is beyond value and will bring praise and honor to our Lord and Savior.

God's blessings are found throughout the entire Bible from Genesis to Revelation. The goal and ultimate blessing is to develop a close relationship with our Lord and Savior. The path to this goal may require trials and hardships that can be physically and emotionally painful.

1 Peter 5:10 reads, "But the God of all grace, who hath called us unto his eternal glory by Christ Jesus, after that ye have suffered a while, make you perfect, stablish, strengthen, settle you."

The Messiah's royal lineage was blessed from the beginning and is detailed in both the book of Mathew and Luke. The book of Mathew details Jesus' genealogy beginning with Abraham and ends with Joseph the husband of Mary. The book of Luke traces Jesus' genealogy back to Adam using Mary's ancestors. In both genealogies Jesus is a direct descendant of King David.

Isaiah 9: 6-7 reads, "For unto us a child is born, unto us a son is given: and the government shall be upon his shoulder: and his name shall be called Wonderful, Counselor, The mighty God, The everlasting father, The Prince of Peace. Of the increase of his government and peace there shall be no end, upon the throne of David, and upon his kingdom, to order it, and to establish it with judgment and with justice from henceforth even for ever. The zeal of the Lord of hosts will perform this."

Introduction

THE GREATEST BLESSING MAN has received has been from God when he gave His only Son so that man's sins may be forgiven and he may enter heaven. God allowed his only Son to be born on this earth as a man to deliver His word and to reveal His love. God's only Son died on the cross and rose to break the seal of death and allow man's soul to escape the penalty of sin.

Isaiah 53:3-5 reads, "He was despised and rejected of men; a man of sorrows, and acquainted with grief: and we hid as it were our faces from him: he was despised, and we esteemed him not. Surely he hath borne our griefs, and carried our sorrows: yet we did esteem him stricken, smitten of God, and afflicted. But he was wounded for our transgressions, he was bruised for our iniquities: the chastisement of our peace was upon him; and with his stripes we are healed."

God's only Son bore the sins of all men as He was tortured and hung crucified on the cross. Jesus Christ was the sacrificial lamb that paid the price for man's sins. This sacrificial blessing is beyond our comprehension and no man is worthy of such a gift.

Ephesians 1:3 reads, "Blessed be the God and Father of our Lord Jesus Christ, who hath blessed us with all spiritual blessings in heavenly places in Christ."

We humbly kneel before our Lord praising His name and thanking Him for all our blessings. We praise and thank our Lord for His Holy Spirit that counsels us, and guides us through each day.

The God we worship is a sovereign God that controls all that occurs within the universe. Our God is immortal, omniscient, and omnipresent, meaning He has always been and will always be present everywhere and is available to each person. Our God is the same today as in the past, and as

Introduction

in the future. There is nothing impossible for God and His control is based on His love.

Our God is a personal God that is interested in each individual. The Bible provides genealogies that list names of each individual both Jew and Gentile that were related to Jesus Christ (the Messiah) and in some cases details how God worked through their lives. These genealogies also confirm the prophecy that Jesus was the Son of David by detailing the name of each person that was an ancestor of Jesus the Messiah. The historical accuracy of the Bible is substantiated by listing all the ancestors of Joseph, Mary, and Jesus starting with Adam.

It is believed that both Mary and Joseph shared the same genealogy from Adam (est. 4223 BC) to King David (est. 1010 BC). It is believed that from that point forward Mary's and Joseph's genealogy changed. Mary the mother of Jesus was a descendant from King David's son, Nathan and Joseph was a descendant of Solomon, another son of King David. A number of verses in both the Old and the New Testament prophesied that the Messiah would be the Son of David. Consequently, Jesus Christ was a descendant by blood of King David from His mother Mary and by adoption from His earthly father Joseph.

Creation
Time unknown

In the beginning God created the heaven and the earth from nothing. He created man from the dust of the ground, and breathed into his nostrils the breath of life. God created woman from a rib of man. Generation after generation of women and men live and die, returning to nothing but dust. Their lives are short and in many cases die without any thought or hope for their souls and the eternal spiritual life with their Creator. They are simply willing to die and ignore the promises in the Bible and its message of salvation.

Genesis 1:1-3 reads, "In the beginning God created the heaven and the earth. And the earth was without form, and void; and darkness was upon the face of the deep. And the Spirit of God moved upon the face of the water. And God said, Let there be light: and there was light."

Genesis 1:21-22 reads, "And God created great whales, and every living creature that moveth, which the waters brought forth abundantly, after that kind: and God saw that it was good. And God blessed them, saying, Be fruitful, and multiply, and fill the waters in the seas, and let fowl multiply in the earth."

Genesis 1:27-28 reads, "So God created man in his own image, in the image of God created he him, male and female created he them. And God blessed them, and God said unto them, Be fruitful, and multiply, and replenish the earth, and subdue it: and have dominion over the fish of the sea, and over the fowl of the air, and over every living thing that moveth upon the earth."

The original sin of man began with Adam and Eve. Satan did tempt them with great riches and power and the promise they would be like God. Genesis 3:5 reads, "For God doth know that in the day ye eat thereof, then your eyes shall be opened, and ye shall be as gods, knowing good and evil." Man is easily puffed up by pride with accomplishments, success, possessions and an endless list of other things. Pride has been in existence before man and is very dangerous and can quickly lead to sin and separation from God as was the case with Satan. Lucifer's pride led him to being cast from heaven. Lucifer became extremely proud of his beauty, intelligence, and power to the point he desired all the glory and not God. Pride, arrogance, and taking on an attitude of superiority are contrary to loving your neighbor as yourself. Pride leads to making comparisons and judging another person (God's creation). Our fallen nature and our own sin makes finding fault in others a pure act of hypocrisy. The Holy Spirit allows believers to discern evil and good and will provide a way to escape evil.

Our sovereign God out of His love, infinite wisdom, and in His time created the heaven and the earth. He created the seas and the land and all the vegetation. And on the sixth day God created man and woman in his image and allowed them to have dominion over all living creatures.

Genesis 1:28 reads, "And God blessed them, and God said unto them, Be fruitful, and multiply, and replenish the earth, and subdue it: and have dominion over the fish of the sea, and over the fowl of the air, and over every living thing that moveth upon the earth."

Genesis 1:31 reads, "And God saw every thing that He had made, and, behold, it was very good. And the evening and the morning were the sixth day." God had created a perfect garden where man could exist and multiply and have dominion over all living creatures. Nothing was denied to man except for the tree of the knowledge of good and evil. This one test of obedience and man's love for God would have eternal consequences. God is a Holy God that cannot tolerate sin. This sin of disobedience by Adam and Eve resulted in punishment and the fall of man. Lucifer was successful in tempting Adam and Eve and allowing to them fall out of favor with God. This perfect garden would turn to a field of thorns and thistles and the ground would be cursed. Man and animals from that time forward would experience suffering and death.

Genesis 2:7 reads, "And the Lord God formed man of the dust of the ground, and breathed into his nostrils the breath of life; and man became a living soul." God breathed into man life and a soul that gave man the ability to worship and commune with God's Holy Spirit. Today man still experience death and suffering, but now has the option to save his soul by accepting God's gift of eternal life and denying his sinful nature. God allows man to suffer the consequences of his sin and at the same time still offers eternal salvation through His Son. Man's sinful nature creates a daily battle with sin that man needs to confront and conquer. God allows us all to suffer the consequences of our sins and the sins of a fallen world for the purpose of instruction. We need to confess all sin and ask for forgiveness for all sin. As Christians we may be singled out, discriminated against, and rejected because of our faith. God allows this type of suffering so we may appreciate the suffering that was experienced by His son, Jesus Christ.

Isaiah 30:18 reads, "And therefore will the Lord wait, that he may be gracious unto you, and therefore will he be exalted, that he may have mercy upon you: for the Lord is a God of judgment: blessed are all they that wait for him."

As we humbly pray to God we ask for the knowledge and strength to run from sin and to run to His grace and mercy. Our Lord and Savior is a God of judgment who loving and graciously longs to show His compassion for those who are faithful and obedient to His word.

It was because of Jesus Christ that we are blessed beyond measure and are now in His family. His blessings allow us to commune with our Father and experience His love and gracious Spirit that permeates our very soul. We are blessed with awareness that God is with us each day and His blessings are beyond our comprehension.

Noah's ark and the flood
(Approximately 2894 BC)

THE WORLD HAD FALLEN into a deep state of depravity with most people being morally corrupt. Satan and his demonic angels had completely overtaken the human race creating untold violence and death. Adam and Eve's disobedience had a devastating impact on all of the human race then and forever. Sin changed the status of man from God's perfect creation to a man fallen in nature. Satan and his demonic angels inflicted unspeakable perversions on man to the point where violence and corruption ruled the day. These perverted angels were chained and cast into darkness prior to the flood to await the judgment (2 Peter 2:4). Men were exceedingly wicked.

All disobedience to God's word results in man's suffering. Suffering is experienced as a result of living in a fallen world infested with disease and death, man's disobedience, and living a life that is not Christ-centered.

For 600 years Noah lived as a righteous man in a society that was completely evil with no hope for salvation. God blessed Noah with incredible courage, strength and determination to complete a project that was viewed as complete folly by all.

2 Peter 3:3-7 reads, "Knowing this first, that there shall come in the last days scoffers, walking after their own lusts. And saying, where is the promise of his coming? For since the fathers fell asleep, all things continue as they were from the beginning of the creation. For this they willingly are ignorant of, that by the word of God the heavens were of old, and the earth standing out of the water and in the water. Whereby the world that then was, being overflowed with water perished: But the heavens and the earth, which are now, by the same word are kept in store, reserved unto fire against the day of judgment and perdition of ungodly men."

Noah's Ark and the Flood

The Apostle Peter in these verses recalled the flood and warned those that scoff and ridicule would be judged and held accountable for every word and their actions.

Noah preached and warned the people that they needed to repent of their sins and prepare for a flood. No one took him seriously and continued with their daily rituals. The same is true today as millions of people continue with their daily lives unresponsive to the message of the Bible.

Psalm 37:9-10 reads, "For evildoers shall be cut off: but those that wait upon the Lord, they shall inherit the earth. For yet a little while, and the wicked shall not be: yea, thou shalt diligently consider his place, and it shall not be."

King David in these verses realized that throughout history the wicked do succeed and survive for a short period of time. However, these periods are short-lived and eventually end in God's time. As believers we place our trust and faith in a sovereign God that is the same today as yesterday, and is the same forever.

Noah was the tenth Patriarch prior to the flood that lived for several centuries. God commanded Noah to build the ark after all the people of the land rejected his message to worship the only true God. God's patience did run out which resulted in God only saving Noah and his sons Shem, Ham, and Japheth, and their wives. God also commanded Noah to build a massive ark and collect animals that would be saved from the flood.

God blessed Noah and his family because he was an obedient, righteous, and blameless servant throughout his entire 600 years of life. It took Noah 120 years to build the ark and during that time he preached to the people about the need to worship God. They refused to believe and responded by saying there was no God. Noah walked with God and listen to God for direction each day and God blessed Noah with safety for his family and another 350 years of life after the flood. Proverbs 8:32 reads, "Now therefore hearken unto me, O ye children: for blessed are they that keep my ways." Listening to God's instruction and following His direction allows us to be wise and receive His blessing. God gave Noah specific instructions (i.e., the type of wood, waterproofing materials) how to build the ark and prepare for the flood. In some ways the situation has not changed. Christians today warn the non-believer of the judgment to come, but in many cases they refuse to listen.

Noah walked in faith and feared God when he built the ark. The people of the world were given the opportunity to believe, but instead brought judgment on themselves with disbelief and dishonoring Noah's message. Noah like all men had a fallen nature with many frailties that caused him and his family much distress.

God is a loving and gracious God who was and is offering salvation to all and is urging all to turn to real repentance. However, man exhausted God's patience when all of man's actions and thoughts were evil which resulted in millions being lost in the flood. God is a righteous and sovereign God who is the same God that Noah followed and is the same God that allowed the flood to occur in a decaying world of evil. We do not know the mind of God and we know that we do not understand all of His plans for us. However, there are verses that address the issue of willful sin.

Hebrews 10:26 reads, "For if we sin willfully after that we have received the knowledge of the truth, there remaineth no more sacrifice for sin."

Hebrews 10:30-31 reads, "For we know him that hath said, VENGENANCE BELONGETH UNTO ME, I will recompense, saith the Lord. And again, THE LORD SHALL JUDGE HIS PEOPLE. It is a fearful thing to fall into the hands of the living God."

As Christians we will all be judged by an all powerful, sovereign God as we stand in front of Him with all of our sins. Those that asked for salvation and later rejected all belief will be judged by God.

APPLICATION

Noah was an ordinary man with many frailties. However, Noah found favor from God and walked with Him because Noah was a righteous man who loved and obeyed God. He was a highly skilled hard working man capable with God's direction of building a massive structure such as the ark. His unweaving obedience and loyalty to God was tested with continual ridicule and harassment by the local community. His skills also included being a farmer and herdsmen. He was also a loving husband and father of three sons and their wives.

God will work through a person by providing inspiration. However, this inspiration will be forgotten if these new creative ideas are not quickly developed. Discipline also plays an important part in the process in developing new ideas and requires skills to be perfected for ideas to be implemented. God will open new doors that will resolve issues and will give direction when goals seem impossible to reach.

Isaiah 58:11 reads, "And the Lord shall guide thee continually, and satisfy thy soul in drought, and make fat thy bones: and thou shalt be like a water garden, and like a spring of water, whose waters fail not."

Proverbs 3:5-6 reads, "Trust in the Lord with all thine heart; and lean not unto thine own understanding. In all thy ways acknowledge him, and he shall direct thy paths."

God is always there to guide us through each step throughout our entire lives. It is our responsibility to share all of our cares and burdens with God each day. We are His creation and He loves us and wants to protect us from harm and to provide for our every need. We are to place our trust in God and to wait patiently for His blessings. God's word has been in place since the beginning of time and will remain in place for eternity. It is the only thing in this universe that does and will not change. Countless numbers of generations have passed and still God's word remains the same. Hundreds of millions can attest that trusting in a loving God and obeying His word in love is the only path to fulfillment. We are all created in His image and we all long to one day to be one with our Creator.

Noah, his sons, and wives were blessed by God and would be the only human beings allowed to survive the flood. This one monumental event would destroy all of mankind and at the same time provide a new start for all of mankind. This was one more example of how Satan has tried to destroy all of mankind and failed. God spared only Noah and his family to ensure that the royal bloodline would continue and that His plan would unfold with the birth of His Son within this royal bloodline.

Abraham and the Covenant
(Approximately 2166–1953 BC)

BLESSINGS FOUND IN THE Old Testament are generally about God's creation, His protection by providing us with our daily provisions, and a prosperous family. However, there were periods of time where God determined men were lost in sin and a new beginning needed to be established for the benefit of mankind. Noah and his family were blessed and selected by God to survive the flood and to begin the re-population of the earth. God at some time later created a covenant with Abraham, his son Isaac, Isaac's son Jacob, and Jacob's twelve sons. The twelve sons of Jacob would be the fathers of the twelve tribes of Israel and the chosen nation of God. God blessed Abraham and the Israelites that established the nation of Israel. They were the people (the Israelites) that finally occupied the Promised Land. This chosen nation of God would serve as a leader to all other nations in following God's word and living as an example of an obedient people. God selected Israel for the primary purpose of being a nation of priests, prophets, and His representative in a world of sinners. Israel's message was the promise of a Savior and Messiah that would come for the salvation of all mankind. Unfortunately, as prophesied many did deny Christ and still today refuse to recognize Jesus as the Messiah and Savior for all of mankind. 1 Peter 2:9 reads, "But ye are a chosen generation, a royal priesthood, a holy nation, a peculiar people; that ye should show forth the praises of him who hath called you out of darkness into his marvelous light."

However, the qualifier is that these blessings are directly related to the entire nation of Israel and not to the individuals. God does bless individuals on an individual basis and those blessings may vary with obedience, God's plan for their lives, and their relationship with their Lord and Savior. God loves His creation (all of mankind) and wants to commune with each one and be part of their daily lives. Galatians 3:28-29 reads, "There is neither Jew nor Greek, there is neither bond nor free, there is neither male nor female: for ye are all one in Christ Jesus. And if ye be Christ's, then are ye Abraham's seed, and heirs according to the promise."

Mankind becomes the children of God by faith in Jesus Christ. Those that are baptized make a public declaration and are sealed into an intimate relationship with their Lord and Savior. This intimate relationship can be one that brings a greater realization of greater responsibility and a position where greater blessings are present.

God called Abraham and told him to settle in the land of Canaan an area that today includes Lebanon, Syria, Jordan, and Israel. Sometime later God appears to Abraham again in the form of three men. Abraham at the age of 100 runs to meet them and bows his face to the ground.

Genesis 18:2-3 reads, "And he lift up his eyes and looked, and, lo, three men stood by him: and when he saw them, he ran to meet them from the tent door, and bowed himself toward the ground. And said, My Lord, if now I have found favor in thy sight, pass not away, I pray thee, from thy servant." Abraham was visited by the Angel of the Lord and two angels for the purpose of blessing him with the message of a son.

The message of a son seemed impossible to Sarah and she laughed in her heart knowing she was too old to bear a child. God again uses another situation to teach us that nothing is impossible with God. This child would be the promised child named Isaac. Isaac would be blessed and inherit all of the land that was given to Abraham.

Abraham was known as a friend of God who actually pleaded and begged God not to destroy Sodom because of those few that were considered to be righteous. God heard Abraham's plea and blessed Abraham when he was allowed to warn Lot, his nephew and his family to leave the city of Sodom. God sent angels to actually pull Lot and his family out of Sodom and Gomorrah before the cities were completely destroyed. This is one more example of God's grace by allowing Lot and his family to escape and God's patience with people who refused to obey His laws and commandments that had fallen in the depths of unspeakable sin. Today we see man's morals decay as his society continues to accept depraved behavior as being normal. The result of this moral degradation has been the destruction of the family unit with many absent fathers and mothers with few moral standards and the resulting anger that is seen in many acts of violence. The respect for self and others has been lost with the refusal to love God, obey God's commands and to love one another.

One of Abraham's greatest lessons was to follow God's request to make the ultimate sacrifice to end his own son's life. God was instructing Abraham by allowing him to experience the pain a father suffers when allowing his son to be offered as a sacrifice. God was allowing Abraham to get some insight as to the amount a suffering God would endure when Jesus Christ His only son would suffer on the cross for the sins of man. God chose Abraham out of a pagan world and blessed him and his descendants as he stepped out in faith and obedience. God demanded that Abraham meet the requirements of faith and obedience for his descendants to be rewarded with the Promised Land. Faith in a sovereign God reduces worry about the future and allows love, kindness, peace to grow, and is self-denying. Faith and obedience are two important requirements from a sovereign God that are consistently repeated throughout the entire Bible.

Genesis 12:2 reads, "And I will make of thee a great nation, and I will bless thee, and make thy name great; and thou shalt be a blessing:"

Genesis 22:15-18 reads, "And the angel of the Lord called unto Abraham out of heaven the second time, And said, By myself have I sworn, saith the Lord, for because thou hast done this thing, and hast not withheld thy son, thine only son. That in blessing I will bless thou, and in multiplying I will multiply thy seed as the stars of the heaven, and as the sand which is upon the seashore; and thy seed shall posses the gate of his enemies. And in thy seed shall all the nations of the earth be blessed; because thou hast obeyed my voice."

Genesis 25:11 reads, "And it came to pass after the death of Abraham, that God blessed his son Isaac; and Isaac dwelt by the well Lahai-roi."

God's blessings were passed from generation to generation. In some cases these blessings unfolded in unpredictable ways. For example, Esau sold his blessings to his twin brother Jacob who in turn deceived his father Isaac to obtain the blessing. However, God disciplined Jacob by allowing many difficulties into Jacob's life that included being deceived by his wife and beaten by an angelic being. Many of these difficulties were created by Jacob and the decisions he made. Likewise, a believer's difficulties may be the result of God's discipline, God's instruction for growing in strength and wisdom, a method for glorifying God (John 9: 1-3), the result of sin passed down from a prior generation (Exodus 20:5), and other reasons known only to God. Making decisions based on self and your own wisdom will not be part of God's plan for your life. God has a plan for each person that will use each person's unique talents.

God's plan and His blessings are perfect and unfold according to His will. All of the difficulties and hardships in a man's life are created by sin in the world, disobedience by man, and lack of faith. A person that has asked Jesus to take control of their life will not be exempt from difficulties and hardships. However, they have been changed in many ways and have been given the gift of eternal life. This transformation involves changing the person's values and goals, realization and appreciation of God's love, and the claiming of the promise of eternal life with our Savior the Lord Jesus Christ. From that point forward the new Christian will view life's difficulties and challenges from the knowledge of knowing that all things work to further God's grace and love. God loves His creation mankind and will naturally bless, instruct, and discipline His children.

Genesis 27:28-29 reads, "Therefore God give thee of the dew of heaven, and the fatness of the earth, and plenty of corn and wine: Let people serve thee, and nations bow down to thee: be Lord over thy brethren, and let thy mother's son bow down to thee: cursed be every one that curseth thee, and blessed be he that blesseth thee."

The family blessing that was passed on from generation to generation was extremely important because it needed to follow the covenant God made with Abraham and the path that lead to the salvation of mankind and the birth of Jesus. These blessings followed a path that was determined by the personal life of Jesus' ancestors and their sin was responsible for preventing many family sons from experiencing God's blessings. For example, Jacob's first born, Reuben, was not considered to be suitable to lead the family and was passed over because of his sin. The fall of man and his sin is a major obstacle for receiving God's blessings. However, for the believer Jesus' death and resurrection removed all sin as far as the east is from the west (Psalm 103:12).

Philippians 3:10 reads, "That I may know him, and the power of his resurrection, and the fellowship of his sufferings, being made conformable unto his death."

Our God is a holy sovereign God who has no sin, and therefore cannot tolerate any unclean spirit. Consequently, for fallen man to commune with God a sacrifice needs to be made that will wash away his sin. God blessed Abraham by allowing him to gain some understanding of the relationship that exists between a sovereign holy God and fallen man.

APPLICATION

God continues the bloodline with the birth of Abraham and his life of love and obedience for the Lord Almighty. It is believed that Abraham was the son of Terah the ninth descendant of Noah. Abraham was born in Mesopotamia but later moved under God's direction to Canaan a land promised to Abraham by God. Abraham was known as the father of all nations and would enjoy a very close relationship with his Creator.

Three angels visited Abraham at the door of his tent for the purpose of explaining that Sarah was going to give birth to Isaac and the destruction of the cities of Sodom and Gomorrah.

Genesis 18:1-2 reads "And the lord appeared unto him in the plans of Mamre: and he sat in the tent door in the heat of the day; And he lift up his eyes and looked, and lo, three men stood by him: and when he saw them, he ran to meet them from the tent door, and bowed himself toward the ground,"

The birth of Isaac was not possible in the eyes of Sarah. We are quick to dismiss what seems to be physically impossible and what we know not to be true from past experiences. We forget nothing is impossible for our Lord and Savior. He has the ability to change the position of the sun and stars and to create an earth more beautiful than words can describe. He can change our lives in many ways and at any time.

Proverbs 3:5-6 reads, "Trust in the Lord with all thine heart; and lean not unto thine own understanding. In all thine ways acknowledge him, and he shall direct thy paths."

Trusting in God requires a willingness to acknowledge we have many limitations and we need God's direction to guide us through life's many struggles. God does provide direction and does answer our prayers. How and by what means He answers our prayers and directs our lives is in many ways beyond our understanding. However, there are those situations where the answers to our prayers are obvious and our souls are given the opportunity to rejoice and mature in thanksgiving.

Another issue that confronts Abraham is the fact that God was going to destroy both the cities of Sodom and Gomorrah because of their wickedness. Abraham was concerned realizing his nephew Lot and his family lived in Sodom. Abraham pleaded with God and tried to save the people of Sodom. However, God could not find ten righteous people in Sodom, consequently the city was destroyed. God was patience with Abraham and listened to his pleads and allowed Lot and his family to escape Sodom.

Genesis 19:15 reads, "And when the morning arose, then the angels hastened Lot, saying, Arise, take thy wife, and thy two daughters, which are here; least thou be consumed in the iniquity of the city."

Genesis 19:24 reads, "Then the Lord rained upon Sodom and upon Gomorrah brimstone and fire from the Lord out of heaven."

God's mercy and patience is great and His rule is always just. The cities of Sodom and Gomorrah had fallen to great depths of sin. The sins committed by the people of Sodom and Gomorrah were grievous and called out for punishment. God considered all of Abraham's pleads and carefully reviewed all the issues before making a decision.

God can and will destroy any city or nation that becomes too evil. The evils of Sodom and Gomorrah were detestable and were too evil to be spoken of.

1 Thessalonians 5:21-23 reads, "Prove all things; hold fast that which is good. Abstain from all appearance of evil. And the very God of peace sanctify you wholly; and I pray God your whole spirit and soul and body be preserved blameless unto the coming of our Lord Jesus Christ."

Abraham was selected by God to be the father of many nations and the instrument for continuing the bloodline for the Messiah. Israel would be only one of many nations.

Genesis 17:3-6 reads, "And Abram fell on his face: and God talked with him, saying, As for me, behold, my covenant is with thee, and thou shalt be a father of many nations. Neither shall thy name any more be called Abram, but they name shall be Abraham; for a father of many nations have I made thee. And I will make thee exceeding fruitful, and I will make nations of thee, and kings shall come out of thee."

The covenant between God and Abraham was a promise that would have an everlasting effect for many generations and would bless all of mankind in many nations.

Genesis 12:3 reads, "And I will bless them that bless thee, and curse him that curseth thee: and in thee shall all families of the earth be blessed."

All the families of the world would be blessed if they took on the faith of Abraham. The covenant between God and Abraham was a promise of blessings that would be centered on the arrival of the Messiah.

Galatians 3:29 reads, "And if ye be Christ's, then are ye Abraham's seed, and heirs according to the promise."

A person who takes on the faith of Abraham will become a spiritual child of Abraham and will experience the blessings of the covenant made between God and Abraham.

The most difficult truth for Abraham to learn was that he was God's creation. God created all of mankind, has complete control over all of mankind, and required Abraham to understand that God was in control of all things including death. Abraham's test came when God asked Abraham to sacrifice his son, Isaac. Abraham followed God's direction and placed his complete trust in God and believed without a doubt that God was in complete control. Abraham's faith was without doubt and was strong enough to withstand any test.

The children of Abraham are all those of many nations that place their faith in God.

John 8:39-40 reads, "They answered and said unto him, Abraham is our father. Jesus saith unto them, If ye were Abraham's children, ye would do the works of Abraham. But now ye seek to kill me, a man that hath told you the truth, which I have heard of God: this did not Abraham."

Abraham was a man of truth, unquestionable integrity, strong faith, and a man that followed God's direction without doubt. Today, the children of Abraham walk in faith and know God's word and obey His commandments. God spoke to Abraham and instructed Abraham how to obey His charge, commandments, statutes, and His laws. God's commandments exposed sin and allowed Abraham and others to live a righteous life.

Genesis 26:5 reads, "Because that Abraham obeyed my voice, and kept my charge, my commandments, my statues, and my laws."

Isaac and Rebekah
(Approximate 2065–1885 BC)

Isaac was Abraham and Sarah's only son. He was a blessing and a miracle from God since Sarah was well past the age of being able to conceive (90 years old). God was in control and was going to ensure and approve the family lineage of His only Son Jesus Christ. God was prepared to unfold many miracles that would ensure a long family heritage of men that would precede the sacred birth of His only Son.

Isaac's sins were similar to the sins of his father Abraham. Both men lied and said that their wives were their sisters for fear they would be killed. Both Sarah and Rebekah were very beautiful women and would be desired by many to possibly be added to a ruler's harem.

Genesis 26: 2-4 reads, "And the Lord appeared unto him, and said, Go not down into Egypt; dwell in the land which I shall tell thee of: Sojourn in this land, and I will be with thee, and will bless thee, for unto thee, and unto thy seed, I will give all these counties, and I will perform the oath which I sware unto Abraham thy father; And I will make thy seed to multiply as the stars of heaven, and give unto thy seed all these countries; and in thy seed shall all the nations of the earth be blessed."

Genesis 26:12-14 reads, "Then Isaac sowed in that land, and received in the same year a hundredfold: and the Lord blessed him. And the man waxed great, and went forward, and grew until he became very great: For he had possession of flocks, and possession of herds, and great store of servants: and Philistines envied him."

Blessings came in the form of property and other blessings. The property was divided equally between the children with the oldest children receiving a double portion. The blessing was given in the form of a prophecy of blessings that would be given to future descendants. Generally, the oldest child received the double portion and was made head of the family. However, if the oldest child fell out of favor the double portion of property and blessings may go to another child. In the case of Abraham, God made a special blessing that would be passed from one generation to another as long as each generation remained faithful to God's word. The descendants of Abraham would become leaders and gain possession of the land of Canaan. More importantly, God's blessing to Abraham would be the birth of His only Son, Jesus Christ as a direct descendant. The birth of Jesus Christ would be a blessing to all nations of the world.

Isaac was a faithful servant to God who never forgot how God provided the sacrifice of a ram as his substitute. In a time when polygamy was common, Isaac took only one wife, Rebekah. As Abraham's wife Sarah, Rebekah was not able to have children. God heard Isaac's prayers for children and God answered their prayers by blessing them with twin sons (Esau and Jacob).

APPLICATION

Isaac was a gift from God to Abraham and Sarah. Isaac would carry the bloodline forward and be an important part of unfolding God's plan for all of mankind. The name Isaac was given by God and means, "he laughed". It seemed impossible to Abraham and Sarah that they could have a child at their advanced age.

Abraham, Isaac, and Jacob were all consider patriarchs because of their close relationship with God and His wilingness to share with each of them His commandments, statutes, and laws. These men were given great responsibility and authority for communicating and enforcing God's commandments and laws.

As Abraham, Isaac followed God's commands and moved to different lands.

Genesis 26:2-3 reads,"And the Lord appeared unto him, and said, Go not down into Egypt; dwell in the land which I shall tell thee of: Sojourn in this land, and I will be with thee, and will bless thee; for unto thee, and unto thy seed, I will give all these counties, and I will perform the oath which I sware unto Abraham thy father;"

God made the same covenant with Isaac as He made with Abraham. God's blessings for Abraham were passed down to Isaac even though Isaac fails with some of the same issues as Abraham. God's love for mankind is a covenant that cannot be broken and is passed down from generation to generation. The conditions are simple and strait forward, as Abraham we must be obedient to God's word and exercise faith in all situations to enjoy the promised blessings.

Jacob the Leah

(Approximate 1836–1689 BC)

THE COVENANT GIVEN BY God to Abraham was passed down to Isaac and then to Jacob and then to his descendants. Jacob was not a perfect man and struggled with sin his entire life. He started his life by cheating Esau out of his birthright and blessing and continued to struggle with God over the control his life. A personal relationship with God will include blessings, instruction, and discipline just as in all relationships there is some conflict. All of the patriarchs sinned, were disobedient and experienced God's loving discipline. Jacob had a dream where God did confirm his covenant with him and his descendants.

Genesis 28: 12-13 reads, "And he dreamed, and behold a ladder set up on earth, and the top of it reached to heaven: and behold the angels of God ascending and descending on it. And, behold, the Lord stood above it, and said, I am the Lord God of Abraham thy father, and the God of Isaac: the land whereon thou liest, to thee will I give it, and thy seed:"

The dream confirms that there was a continual movement of angels between heaven and earth and that Jacob was under God's protection at all times.

Jacob at the age of 130 had to make the most difficult decision of his life. He had moved his family to Canaan the land that had been promised to his family since the time of Abraham. Unfortunately, there was a great famine in the land and people were starving. To further complicate the issue Jacob discovered that Joseph his son was not dead, but living in Egypt under the protection of the Pharaoh. Jacob also received an invitation and a cart of gifts from Joseph to join him in Egypt. Jacob needed God's direction and he prayed that God would answer his prayer.

Genesis 46:1-4 reads, "And Israel took his journey with all that he had, and came to Beer-sheda, and offered sacrifices unto the God of his father Isaac. And God spake unto Israel in the visions of the night, and said, Jacob, Jacob. And he said, Here am I. And he said, I am God, the God of thy father: fear not go down to Egypt; for I will there make of thee a great nation: I will go down with thee into Egypt; and I will also surely bring thee up again: and Joseph shall put his hand upon thine eyes. "

God answered Jacob's prayer in a way that provided specific directions as to where to go and that He would provide protection on the long journey. Jacob travel to Egypt during a drought that would last more than seven years. He travelled with his eleven sons, wives, children along with their herds of cattle, sheep, and goats. They were greeted in Egypt by Joseph and were given rich fertile land to work, allowed to manage the Pharaoh's livestock, and Jacob's family grew and thrived.

Genesis 46: 29-30, reads, "And Joseph made ready his chariot, and went up to meet Israel his father, to Goshen, and presented himself unto him; and he fell on his neck, and wept on his neck a good while. And Israel said unto Joseph, Now let me die, since I have seen thy face, because thou art yet alive."

The drought brought about severe hardship to all the people of the region to the point where many were starving and selling all they had for food to survive. It was Joseph and his wisdom that provided for a great storage of grain that allowed many to survive the famine.

Joseph was a son that was hated by his brothers, beaten and sold to a passing caravan. God would use this despised and rejected man to accomplish great things and to be the answer to Jacob's prayer. God brought about a miracle by taking a slave called Joseph left for dead and placing him in a position that ensured that God's man Jacob and the twelve tribes of Jacob would survive in great numbers.

Both Jacob and Joseph placed their trust in God and asked for His direction. God answered their prayers by providing His loving grace in His time and in His way. The message is clear, if you live a life that is based on your wisdom you will not experience God's plan for your life. God will not fail to unfold his promises regardless of the circumstance. No one would expect a beaten slave left for dead to be an important part of a sovereign God's plan for all of mankind. God's plan for the world will unfold regardless of our individual values or situations. Today, many are enslaved to earthly values and their entire existence is focused on self.

It is God's grace that blesses us with promises that we do not deserve. Jacob took every decision to God in prayer. Jacob was blessed greatly because of his faithfulness in taking all decisions to God in prayer. His life was based on God's wisdom and not his own wisdom. Jacob and his twelve sons all prospered in Egypt and raised twelve great family tribes.

2 Samuel 7:28 reads, "And now, O Lord God, thou art that God, and thy words be true, and thou hast promised this goodness unto thy servant."

We are the creation of a sovereign all powerful God that has no sin and cannot tolerant any sin. He is a loving patience God that has given His only Son as a sacrifice for all of man's sin so that man may commune with God his Creator. Jacob was living out God's plan for his life and the life of his family that included traveling and moving his family to Egypt. Obedience in our daily life pleases God and allows us to receive His blessing. However, disobedience will bring discipline to those that are faithful servants. We belong to a loving, faithful God who will never fail to provide for His faithful servants.

APPLICATION

Esau was not interested in his birthright and was willing to sell it to Jacob for a bowl of stew. Jacob on the other hand, realized the value and importance of the bloodline and was willing to assume all the responsibility and authority associated with the birthright. Unfortunately, when Isaac was on his deathbed and ready to give the final blessing, Jacob with the aid of Rebekah, Isaac's wife, devised a plan to deceive Isaac.

Regardless of the conflict and the many sins between Jacob, Esau, and the family, God's plan would be unfolded.

Genesis 25:23 reads, "And the Lord said unto her, two nations are in thy womb, and two manner of people shall be separated from the bowels; and the one people shall be stronger than the other people; and the elder shall serve the younger."

Jacob being the youngest son would be the son to carry the bloodline for the Son of David, Jesus the Christ. God has a plan for each person and regardless of the number of bad decisions we make He is always there to comfort us and to forgive us our many sins.

Jacob was a deceitful and crafty man that relied on his own skills to resolve issues he encountered. His deception and lies to Isaac resulted in Esau's wrath and pledge to kill Jacob. All of Jacob's efforts to resolve issues ended in failure and the wrath of his victims. Men are generally more inclined to try to resolve issues on their own rather than to pray and patiently wait on God for His answer. Jacob was in a difficult situation with his brother coming in the morning with 400 men to kill him and others to do him harm. Jacob spent the night struggling and wrestling with an angel of God.

Jacob was full of fear and dreaded the meeting with his brother Esau and realized he needed God's blessing to change his life and resolve all of his conflicts. In complete desperation he told the angel he wasn't going to release him unless he was blessed.

Genesis 32:26-29 reads, "And he said, Let me go, for the day breaketh. And he said, I will not let thee go, except thou bless me. And he said unto him, What is thy name? And he said Jacob. And he said, Thy name shall be called no more Jacob, but Israel: for as a prince hast thou power with God and with men, and hast prevailed. And Jacob asked him, and said, Tell me, I pray thee, thy name? And he blessed him there."

The encounter with the angel made Jacob physically vulnerable with an injured hip and at the same time required that he be more dependent on faith. God's blessing changed Jacob from being a man who tried to resolve all issues with lies and deception to a man who was completely dependent on God for all things. Jacob's struggle with the angel pleased God and resulted in Jacob getting the blessing he fought for. We all struggle and wrestle with difficult issues throughout our lives. The sooner we realize our limitations, the sooner we place a greater trust in God's love, and wisdom, the sooner we live a fuller and joy filled life. We continue in a life of prayer and patiently wait on the Lord for His direction and answer to our needs. God answers our prayers in many different ways and in some ways we do not understand. For example, God will wait until the time is right for an issue to be resolved. The right time could be dependent on other people, an individual's maturity, experiences to be realized, knowledge of the issues, and countless other aspects of daily life.

Judah and Tamar
(Approximately 1755–1676 BC)

JACOB HAD TWELVE SONS. Jacob and his wife Leah's sons were Reuben, Simeon, Levi, Judah, Issachar, and Zebulun. Jacob and his wife Rachel sons were Joseph and Benjamin. He also had sons with Zipah (Gad, Asher) and Bilaha (Dan, Naphtali). Reuben was the oldest son and would have normally been given the double portion of land and the family blessing; however, because of his involvement in the selling of Joseph to a caravan, he was denied that inheritance.

Jacob would bless all twelve sons by giving them all some portion of the Promised Land which now includes all of Israel. Jacob under God's direction singled out Judah the forth son for the most prominent blessing. Jacob's son Levi and his sons would become priests and would be responsible for keeping and maintaining the law for all the tribes.

However, Judah hated his brother Joseph and was involved along with his brothers in the selling of his brother Joseph. This sin caused Judah a great deal of suffering over the next twenty years with his wife and sons. Two of Judah's sons lost their lives because of their sin and disobedience. Judah's third son Shelah was too young and did not marry Tamar the chosen wife for Judah's first son Er. Tamar changed her appearance and tricked Judah into having a relationship that resulted in the birth of twins. The child named Perez was the first born and was in the genealogy line that God delivered His promise and blessing for all of mankind.

The tribe of Judah was blessed and grew to great strength and was the law giver for all the tribes of Israel. Judah was a strong warrior with a strong character and determination to follow God's plan for Israel. It was the tribe of Judah's numbers and strength that allowed them to be aggressive in driving out the Canaanites. In addition, Judah's strength allowed him to move

Judah and Tamar

the tabernacle from Shiloh to Mount Zion. Mount Zion is located on an eastern hill in the city of Jerusalem. Jerusalem was the capital of the southern kingdom of Israel, Judah.

Genesis 49:8-10 reads, "Judah, thou art he whom thy breather shall praise: thy hand shall be in the neck of thy enemies; thy father's children shall bow down before thee. Judah is a lion's whelp: from the prey, my son, thou art gone up: he stooped down, he couched as a lion, and as an old lion; who shall rouse him up? The scepter shall not depart from Judah, nor a lawgiver from between his feet, until Shiloh come; and unto him the gathering of the people be."

Judah was held in high esteem as the fourth son of Jacob and Leah. Judah took on a leadership role of Jacob's family and negotiated a smooth transition into the land of Goshen (eastern part of the delta of the Nile). Jacob predicted that the tribe of Judah would grow to have superior power over the other tribes and grow in prosperity. It was the tribe of Judah after the enslavement in Egypt that was able to unify the Hebrew people of Israel. The tribe of Judah preserved the true religion, maintained and preserved the priesthood, and ensured the ceremonies of the temple.

It was promised that the Messiah for all of mankind would be from the tribe of Judah and the Son of David.

Isaiah 9:6-7 reads, "For unto us a child is born, unto us a son is given: and the government shall be upon his shoulder: and his name shall be called Wonderful, Counselor, The mighty God, The everlasting Father, The Prince of Peace. Of the increase of his government and peace there shall be no end, and upon the throne of David, and upon his kingdom, to order it, and upon his kingdom, or order it, and to establish it with judgment and with justice from henceforth even for ever. The zeal of the Lord of hosts will perform this."

Jacob would move his twelve sons and their families (est. 70 members) to Goshen that was part of the Nile delta in Egypt. He meets Joseph in Goshen in about 1660 BC.

Judah was the fourth son of Jacob and was chosen by God to carry on the genealogy line of the Messiah. However, Joseph the son of Jacob and Rachel was also a righteous man that lived a godly life and was also blessed. Joseph was Jacob's favorite son and received the family blessings because of his father's love and because of how he was treated by his brothers. Joseph was hated by his brothers who sold him into slavery. Jacob also blessed Josephs' sons Ephraim and Manasseh. In this situation sin was the major obstacle in preventing the first born Reuben or many of his brothers from receiving the family blessing. Sin cannot be under estimated. Sin is extremely dangerous and clever and is always looking for an opportunity to creep into and destroy a persons' life.

Genesis 50:18-20 reads, "And his brethren also went and fell down before his face, and they said, Behold, we be thy servants. And Joseph said unto them, fear not: for am I in the place of God? But as for you, ye thought evil against me; but God meant it unto good, to bring to pass, as it is this day, to save much people alive."

Joseph was hated by his brothers, was thrown into a pit and later sold to a caravan. Joseph ended up in Egypt as a slave. After many years in Egypt and many difficulties Joseph eventually rose to a position of great responsibility. Many years later he met his brothers again. However, at this time Joseph was in control and could have easily taken revenge against his brothers for being sold into slavery. God had blessed Joseph and had changed his character. Joseph realized God was responsible for his blessings and success and that his position was for the purpose of helping others. Consequently, he fed his brothers and cared for them. God's blessings in this case carried the responsibility of caring for others.

There was a great famine that caused Jacob and his twelve sons to migrate to Egypt. Joseph had been in Egypt for many years and became reunited with his family. The families quickly grew in numbers and were forced into ruthless labor by the Egyptians. It is believed that Joseph and all of his brothers died in Egypt. However, the twelve tribes of Jacob grew in great numbers and were able to flourish in the lush delta of the Nile in spite of the harsh treatment under slave labor.

APPLICATION

Jacob called all his sons together during his last days for the purpose of delivering his blessing to Judah.

Genesis 49:8-9 reads, "Judah, thou art he whom thy brethren shall praise: thy hand shall be in the neck of thine enemies; thy father's children shall bow down before thee. Judah is a lion whelp: from the prey, my son, thou art gone up: he stooped down, he couched as a lion, and as an old lion; who shall rouse him up?"

Judah was no ordinary man. It is believed that Judah was an extremely strong man capable of throwing large rocks that would knock a soldier off his horse. He was also a fierce warrior that caused his enemies to flee rather than engage in battle. From that time forward the tribe of Judah would be symbolized by a lion.

Even though Judah was a fierce warrior and was compared to a lion, he was also aware of his failures and was willing to share these failures with his children. He was able share his love with his children by teaching them to avoid what the world considers important. Our children are God's gifts to us to be treasured and prepared for a meaningful life centered on praising and worshipping their Messiah and Lord.

As parents it is important that we are honest and share our success and failures with our children. Raising children today is extremely difficult due to the lack of morals and Christian values that are missing in almost every aspect of our daily life. It is not uncommon to hear of school teachers that have been sexually involved with their students and for students to kill teachers and other students. Children are not being taught Christian values and morals and consequently do not know the difference between good and evil. They are easily influenced by their peers and follow those they see as role models.

Unfortunately, society will continue to deteriorate as more continue to view religion as dogma and spirituality is ignored by the public schools. The result is that we have children being raised in our society without any spiritual guidance from the home or in the public schools.

Fifty years ago we did not have children killing children. In fact, children fifty years ago were allowed to join school gun clubs and shoot at the school's gun range without concern for a child's safety. So, how did society deteriorate to the point where some children have no regard for their own life or the life of another person? Fifty years ago children did not have access to the internet and the huge collection of uncensored information. Television was in most homes but subject to heavy censorship if material was considered objectionable, harmful to children, and morally degrading. Today, those moral requirements are no longer enforced and children are exposed to all types of violence and immorality at a young age on the television or on the internet. The combination of the deterioration of the family unit, exposure to decades of immorality on the TV and the internet, and no spiritual education has resulted in a greater number of children with no respect for themselves or for other children and life itself. It is critical that young impressionable minds be protected from the perverse ideology of today's society. Children are easily convinced to follow and will copy behavior they see on the internet and other uncensored media.

Those that are responsible and guilty of destroying the innocence of young minds will pay a heavy price on judgment day.

Jesus Christ is also referred to as the lion of Judah and the root of David.

Revelations 5:5 reads, "And one of the elders saith unto me, Weep not: behold, the lion of the tribe of Judah, the root of David, hath prevailed to open the book, and loose the seven seals thereof."

Jesus Christ alone has absolute control and has the power to open the seven seals and to judge and rule. Jesus Christ was a descendent of David and with devastating force will bring judgment upon the earth.

Jesus Christ was the lamb that was sacrificed for all of our sins and is the only one that has the authority to break the seals of judgment upon His return. He alone with God the Father sits on the throne that provides the sure foundation that each Christian builds his faith in hopes of eternity. A Christian's faith is built on God's promise to provide the safety that will be needed by all on Judgment day.

Perez and wife unknown
(Approx. 1663–1573 BC)

Perez was the first born of Judah and Tamar. He also had a twin brother named Zerah.

Ruth 4:12 reads, "And let thy house be like the house of Pharez, whom Tamar bare unto Judah, of the seed which the Lord shall give thee of this young woman."

Perez was blessed greatly with the honor of carrying on the lineage of Judah. This blessing was remembered by the Jewish people as a blessing that was beyond measure. In addition, not only did Perez carry on the line of Judah, he was also an eminent part in carrying on the lineage of the Messiah. Some 1700 years later Jesus Christ would be born from this lineage as a child from the tribe of Judah.

It is believed that during this time period Joseph and all of his brothers died in Egypt. However, the children of Israel grew in great numbers and they became a strong force for the Egyptians to contend with. The Egyptians became fearful of a possible revolt and therefore inflicted heavy workloads to prevent them from rebelling. The Pharaoh decided that the best way to slow the population growth of the Hebrews was to kill all male babies.

Genesis 49:10 reads, "The scepter shall not depart from Judah, nor a lawgiver from between his feet, until Shiloh come, and unto him shall the gathering of the people be."

The tribe of Judah was blessed with royal power and grew to great strength and outnumbered all other tribes. It was the tribe of Judah that led all other tribes through the wilderness. The Messiah would come from this prosperous tribe along with King David and Solomon.

APPLICATION

The blessing of Perez is that God will allow you to breakthrough every barrier to fulfill His purpose and His will for your life. Even if things are not currently working out the way you had hoped, God is still anointing you and clearing a path for your life.

Psalm 42:8 reads, "Yet the Lord will command his loving-kindness in the daytime, and in the night his song shall be with me, and my prayers unto the God of my life."

Psalm 43:3 reads, "O send out thy light and thy truth: let them lead me; let them bring me unto thy holy hill, and to thy tabernacles."

Psalm 78:14 reads, "In the daytime also he led them with a cloud, and all night with a light of fire."

Christians are anointed with the Holy Spirit. The Holy Spirit actually permeates a person's soul and begins a lifelong communion that provides direction and confidence. This anointment by the Holy Spirit also gives the Christian the joy in knowing God is with them each step they take. No barrier can stand against God. No matter the situation, a Christian can take comfort in God's promise that He will always be there for them. A Christian will respond to this divine promise with endless rejoicing, prayers praising His name, and giving thanks for all of His blessings.

Philippians 4:6-7 reads, "Be careful for nothing; but in every thing by prayer and supplication with thanksgiving let your requests be made known unto God. And the peace of God, which passeth all understanding, shall keep your hearts and minds through Christ Jesus."

Psalm 115: 5 reads, "They have mouths, but they speak not, eyes have they, but they see not:"

The anointment of the Holy Spirit also gives a person's heart a fuller vision, an appreciation of God's grace and the gift of His Son, His many blessings, the gift of life, the love for obeying God's commands, and the importance of following His direction. The importance of each Christian's life cannot be under estimated.

Hezron and wife unknown
(Approx. 1593–1503 BC)

THIS IS A TIME period when the population of the Israelites was growing rapidly and a number of Patriarchs were dying. Levi was believed to have lived 137 years and died in about 1590 BC. Levi was Jacob's third son that later became the Levi tribe of Priests. In about 1571 BC Moses was born; found by the Pharaoh's daughter, and began his life in Egypt. Moses in about 1531 BC killed an Egyptian guard and fled Egypt.

Gen 46:12 reads, "And the sons of Judah; Er, and Onan, and Shelh, and Pharez, and Zarah: but Er and Onan died in the land of Canaan. And the sons of Pharez were Hezron and Hamul."

Ruth 4:18 reads, "Now these are the generations of Pharez: Pharez begat Hezron."

Moses fled to the land of Midian and marries Zipporah the daughter of a local priest and land owner. Moses became a shepherd for his father-in-law and spends many years wandering in the desert.

APPLICATION

It is believed that Hezron (son of Perez) was appointed by Moses under God's direction as Prince of the tribe of Judah. It is also believed that Hezron was the leader of the tribe of Judah during the time when Moses led the Israelites out of Egypt and died in the wilderness.

Hezron was chosen by God to be the leader of the tribe of Judah just as his father Perez and his grandfather Judah were chosen by God to be leaders. God's plan included these men as well as many others to unfold God's plan and the bloodline for the Messiah. These men were chosen by God and not self-appointed or planned to be leaders.

Moses was the meekest man on earth and felt he would never possess the qualities needed to be a leader. Yet, God molded him into one of the greatest leaders of all times.

Numbers 12:3 reads, "Now the man Moses was very meek, above all the men which were upon the face of the earth."

God found Moses in the wilderness herding his father-in-law's sheep. When God spoke to Moses he had a number of reasons or excuses why he should not be used to lead the Israelites out of Egypt. God did listen to Moses' concerns and allowed his brother Aaron to travel with him and provide support.

Meekness is a basic requirement that God demands from all His leaders. No leader chosen by God will take pride in his abilities to lead God's people. Leaders chosen by God realize that God is in control in all situations and at all times.

1 Samuel 16:7 reads, "But the Lord said unto Samuel, Look not on his countenance or the height of his stature; because I have refused him: for the Lord seeth not as man seeth; for man looketh on the outward appearance, but the Lord looketh on the heart."

It is believed that Hezron was the leader of the tribe of Judah during the time that Moses led the Jewish people out of Egypt. Leading an estimated 600,000 people and their families would have been an extremely difficult task. God would have chosen Hezron for his management skills, his ability to work with and take direction from Moses, and his relationship with God. Hezron understood he needed to take direction from Moses and to serve him as God's representative.

1 Peter 5:5-6 reads, "Likewise, ye younger, submit yourselves unto the elder. Yea, all of you be subject one to another, and be clothed with humility: for God resisteth the proud, and giveth grace to the humble. Humble yourselves therefore under the mighty hand of God, that he may exalt you in due time:"

A good leader seeks God's direction first and lets God establish the direction and the steps to be taken. The purpose and manner in which this task should be completed should be committed to pleasing God. A life committed in the service to God will be a life lived in reverence and in respect for God and His commandments. The fear of God and a willing spirit is a requirement that must be met first each day.

A life that is involved in serving God is a life that involves sacrifice. God established the model for the Christian's life when He sacrificed His only Son for all of man's sins. A Christian is a servant locked in the battle for the souls of mankind.

Luke 17:10 reads, "So likewise, ye, when ye shall have done all those things which are commanded you, say, We are unprofitable servants, we have done that which was our duty to do."

Following God's commands is the minimum requirement for a faithful servant. Unfortunately, the minimum requirement to be a servant of God is not being met by many. To make matters worse, many churches and seminaries today are not following God's commands and in some cases are distorting God's word to meet cultural pressures.

Ram and wife unknown
(Approx. 1587–1450 BC)

THERE IS NOT A great deal written about Ram other than the fact he was from the tribe of Judah and in the lineage of the Messiah, Jesus Christ.

The ten plagues were believed to have occurred starting in about 1463 BC and ending with the exodus in 1462 BC. The Passover occurred a day prior to the exodus.

Chronicles 2:9 reads, "The sons also of Hezron, that were born unto him: Jerahmeel and Ram, and Chelubai."

Ram was born in Egypt after Jacob migrated the twelve tribes to Goshen (the Nile delta). Ram is only mentioned in a few verses and is referred to be a part of the family lineage of Jesus.

It is also believed that Ram was alive during the time of Moses and the exodus from Egypt. He would have been a leader of the tribe of Judah and a confidant of Moses and Aaron.

Moses (approx. 1527-1407 BC) was from the tribe of Levi and lived during the time the Israelites were enslaved in Egypt. It is believed that Moses was the author of the first five books of the Old Testament; Genesis, Exodus, Leviticus, Numbers, and Deuteronomy. These five books are also included in the Christian Bible, the Jewish Torah and in other religious documents.

Mark 12:26 reads, "And as touching the dead, that they rise: have ye not read in the book of Moses, how in the bush God spake unto him, saying, I am the God of Abraham, and the God of Isaac, and the God of Jacob." God recognized Moses as the author of the books of Moses and refers to the burning bush found in Exodus 3:6.

God's blessings for man are found in the first book of the Bible and continue throughout the entire Bible. In Genesis, God creates the world and the first man and woman. Both man and woman failed to keep God's laws and were almost completely destroyed in a flood. Noah and his family were the only ones to survive the flood and to start a new generation. Later, God continued to bless man with a covenant with Abraham and his descendants (Isaac and Jacob).

Genesis 1:28 reads, "And God blessed them, and God said unto them, Be fruitful, and multiply, and replenish the earth, and subdue it: and have dominion over the fish of the sea, and over the fowl of the air, and over every living thing that moveth upon the earth."

Genesis 9:1 reads, "And God blessed Noah and his sons, and said unto them, Be fruitful, and multiply, and replenish the earth."

Moses was a man of God. God molded Moses into the humblest man on earth so that he may be acceptable as a vessel to be used by God in unfolding many of God's miracles. God also infused into Moses great courage so that great miracles were accomplished. Man is a vessel that can be filled by God's Spirit, but only to the degree that he is free from sin. Self love and pride can be a major obstacle in allowing man to realize greater blessings from God. We have free will that allows us to make decisions based on whether we allow good or evil in our daily lives. It is important that we identify both God's blessings and Satan's evil in our daily lives and ask for forgiveness and the strength to push sin out each day. Moses was not free of sin and struggled with his anger throughout his life. His sin cost him dearly as he was not allowed to enter the promise land. As Moses, we may experience the penalty for our sin in some form (e.g. discipline) at some time and at some point in our life. God will discipline His children because of His love for us just as we discipline our children in love. However, a belief and confession of faith will allow us to spend eternity in heaven with our Lord even though we are all fallen in nature and will face our Lord and God for the judgment for our sins.

God heard the prayers of the Jewish people who were brutally enslaved in Egypt and blessed them by allowing for a means of escape. Moses in the book of Exodus explains how the Israelites were enslaved in Egypt and were released by Pharaoh after God sent 10 terrible plagues that destroyed the land and Pharaoh's rule. The Israelites escaped their bondage by following Moses through the wilderness for the next 40 years. While in the wilderness God provides the Israelites with the 10 commandments and made a covenant with the Israelites that if they follow these laws they would be given Canaan the promised land. Moses' appearance and character was transformed after spending time with God on the mountain.

Exodus 15:13 reads, "Thou in thy mercy hast led forth the people which thou hast redeemed: thou hast guided them in thy strength unto thy holy habitation."

Exodus 15:26 reads, "And said, If thou wilt diligently hearken to the voice of the Lord thy God, and wilt do that which is right in his sight, and wilt give ear to his commandments, and keep all his statues, I will put none of these diseases upon thee, which I have brought upon the Egyptians: for I am the Lord that healeth thee."

Exodus 23:25 reads, "And ye shall serve the Lord your God, and he shall bless thy bread, and thy water; and I will take sickness away from the midst of thee."

Exodus 33:17 reads, "And the Lord said unto Moses, I will do this thing also that thou hast spoken: for thou hast found grace in my sight, and I know thee by name."

Exodus 34:5-7 reads, "And the Lord descended in the cloud, and stood with him there, and proclaimed the name of the Lord. And the Lord passed by before him, and proclaimed, The Lord, The Lord God, merciful and gracious, long-suffering, and abundant in goodness and truth. Keeping mercy for thousands, forgiving iniquity and transgression and sins, and that will by no means clear the guilty; visiting the iniquity of the fathers upon the children, and upon the children's children, unto the third and to the fourth generation."

In this situation God's blessings were given in a number of different forms. God heard the prayers of the Jewish people and He lost patience with the Egyptian Pharaoh. The consequence was that God's wrath virtually destroyed Egypt by destroying the Pharaohs' credibility and status as a God. His military was lost at the bottom of the Red Sea, all the food, livestock, and crops were destroyed and the Egyptian people suffered from many types of diseases. God reacted to the Jewish people's prayers and blessed His people by providing for their freedom and the promise to fulfill the covenant of a promised land. Prayer is an extremely important key to receiving blessings from God. All things are possible with God.

God at one point was contemplating the destruction of all of the Jewish people because of their disobedience in building a gold idol. The worship of idols will provoke the wrath of God.

Exodus 32:10 reads, "Now therefore let me alone that my wrath may wax hot against them, and that I may consume them: and I will make of thee a great nation."

It was only because of Moses' prayers, pleading, and begging that God spared the Israelites from complete destruction. Moses sited the promises and covenants God made with Abraham, Isaac, and Israel that their seed would multiply as the stars of heaven.

Today man's worship of self and man's achievements has created a man that is full of pride and self worship. The worship of man, his achievements and knowledge has left a man that is void of any soul or moral compass. Man's idol is himself and his ability to explain all blessings as manmade and created by man. Satan's fall was due to his love of self and the miracles he could perform. His pride grew like a cancer that resulted in him challenging God and receiving God's wrath. Man's refusal to acknowledge God's blessings will end in the wrath of God for all those who refuse to accept and believe in God and His Son.

We worship a just and sovereign God who hates sin and has invoked His wrath in the past. God is also extremely patient, loving and has showed His mercy and grace in many ways. Unfortunately, our daily lives are engulfed in sin that needs continual prayer. The importance of prayer and confession cannot be stressed enough. A Christian's life begins with the belief and trust in God's only Son, Jesus.

God loves man and His creation and wants to bless us in our daily lives. However, God will not tolerate sin and will not commune with those who are involved in sin. The book of Leviticus defines what is holy and what actions need to be taken to maintain a holy relationship with God. Exodus 19:6 reads, "And ye shall be unto me a kingdom of priests, and a holy nation. These are the words which thou shalt speak unto the children of Israel." Israel became a great nation because its people honored and obeyed God's laws. God in Leviticus explains to the Israelites how to worship God and how to conduct themselves around the Tabernacle. God requires man to be obedient to His word and to honor Him in their words, actions, and worship.

Aaron was Moses' brother and the first high priest for God's people. He accompanied Moses as they both confronted Pharaoh for the release of the Israelites from slavery. Aaron was also allowed access to God and shared with Moses God's instruction for leading the Israelites to be a holy country and a kingdom of priests. It is difficult to understand why Aaron a man who had experienced God's miracles and blessing first hand had failed God so miserably. Moses left the Israelites to pray in the mountains and did not return for a number of weeks. The Israelites determined that Moses had died and that God had left them. Unfortunately, out of grief and fear the Israelites fell back into idol worship. The Israelites again and again fell into the same pattern of blessings, disobedience, discipline, confession, and blessings. In this case Aaron's disobedience resulted in Aaron losing two sons and being denied access to the Promised Land. In fact, both Moses and Aaron sinned against God and both were not allowed to enter the Promised Land. Moses could not control his temper and Aaron lost his faith realizing Moses may not return. Today, Christians fall into the same pattern as they are blessed, sin and fall short of fulfilling God's plan for their lives. God has a unique plan for each individual just as He had a unique plan for Moses and Aaron. A Christian's life is centered on being open and willing to follow God's plan for their life.

Leviticus 9:22 reads, "And Aaron lifted up his hand toward the people, and blessed them, and came down from offering of the sin offering, and the burnt offering, and peace offerings."

Blessings were received by the people from Aaron because of their offerings. The people recognized and identified their sin and were willing to make a sacrifice. They were making a public declaration of their sin with their type of offering. We no longer make public sacrifices for our sins because of the ultimate sacrifice by God's only Son Jesus the Christ. However, it is still important to identify our sins and ask forgiveness through prayer. Sin that is not confessed will work as a block in receiving God's blessings.

The act of making sacrifices was first recorded with Cain and Abel. The dangers of sin cannot be minimized and its disastrous effects cannot be underestimated. God instructed His people that sin came with a cost and that the more severe the sin the greater the cost. Unfortunately, the temple and its priests took advantage of this practice and began selling animals and birds for sacrifices. They became money changers and took advantage of the poor by making a profit on the sale of animals for sacrifice. God ended this practice of animal sacrifices by providing His only Son as the final sacrifice for all sin for whosoever believes in Jesus Christ and His Death and Resurrection. For the non-believing Jews the act of making sacrifices ended in 70 AD when the temple in Jerusalem was destroyed.

Leviticus 25:21 reads, "Then I will command my blessing upon you in the sixth year, and it shall bring forth fruit for three years."

Leviticus 26:3-13 reads, "If ye walk in my statutes, and keep my commandments, and do them; Then I will give you rain in due season, and the land shall yield her increase, and the trees of the field shall yield their fruit. And your threshing shall reach unto the vintage, and the vintage shall reach unto the sowing time: and ye shall eat your bread to the full, and dwell in your land safely. And I will give peace in the land, and ye shall lie down, and none shall make you afraid: and I will rid evil beasts out of the land, neither shall the sword go through your land. And ye shall chase your enemies, and they shall fall before you by the sword. And five of you chase a hundred, and a hundred of you shall put ten thousand to flight: and your enemies shall fall before you by the sword."

Our Creator is a Sovereign God who has considered every aspect of our daily life. The days and nights are measured to provide the right amount of sunlight and rain to grow enough food to feed all on this planet. We have been given dominion over all animals to be used for our purposes. For those who are believers He has given them protection and a way of escape from those who wish harm. Our Creator has seen generation after generation of those who had no thought of thankfulness for God's love or the overwhelming beauty of this planet and its riches. God is a loving, gracious Creator whose patience is beyond measure and whose wrath is unpredicable and disastrous.

The book of Numbers reveals the importance of holiness, worship, and faithfulness. It also discusses how God responded when the Israelites did not take possession of the Promised Land. God condemned them to death in the wilderness and only allowed the next generation to enter the Promised Land. God's judgment can be swift.

The book of Numbers also provides great detail about handling the Ark of the Covenant, the tribes, and the role of priests. God loves His people greatly, but will not tolerate sin and requires all to follow His commandments without hesitation and without complaining. The relationship between God and man is similar to the relationship between a parent and child. However, depending on the type and degree of disobedience God may shorten a man's life. It is believed that 15,000 Israelites lost their lives due to their complaining and disagreements with Moses and Aaron's rule. The relationship between God and Man is loving, but can result in severe consequences if man exhausts God's patience. Leviticus 26:18 reads, "And if ye will not yet for all this hearken unto me, then I will punish you seven times more for your sins." God will bring man to his knees in love and as a blessing.

Numbers 6:22-27 reads, "And the Lord spake unto Moses, saying, Speak unto Aaron and unto his sons, saying, On this wise ye shall bless the children of Israel, saying unto them, the Lord bless thee, and keep, thee: The Lord make his face shine upon thee, and be gracious unto thee: The Lord lift up his countenances upon thee, and give thee peace. And they shall put my name upon the children of Israel; and I will bless them."

God clearly stated He wishes to put His name upon His people so that they may experience His blessings. God will keep His people from danger, bless them, and give them peace.

The book of Deuteronomy is one of the most quoted books in the Old Testament. The book reminds the reader that the Israelites were a chosen people. Deuteronomy 7:6 reads, "For thou art a holy people unto the Lord thy God: the Lord thy God hath chosen thee to be a special people unto himself, above all people that are upon the face of the earth." This declaration by God that the Israelites were a chosen people carried a great deal of responsibility and would be completely void of pride.

The book of Deuteronomy also outlines the relationship between God and the Israelites as they entered the Promised Land. The relationship between God and the Israelites was always loving with loving discipline. God would only allow those to continue with the journey if they continually obeyed the Ten Commandments. If they fell back to worshiping pagan gods they would perish.

Obedience to God's word is a requirement for blessing to continue. In other words, if you are disobedient to God's word blessings will be withheld. Our lives are measured in years, months, weeks, days, hours, and minutes. We will be held accountable for this short period of time and need to ensure we spend these days, hours, and minutes wisely. Obviously, being involved or associated with sin during this time period would be the worst option.

Deuteronomy 7:13 reads, "And he will love thee, and bless thee, and multiply thee; he will also bless the fruit of thy womb, and the fruit of thy land, thy corn, and thy wine, and the thine oil, the increase of thy kine, and the flocks of thy sheep, in the land which he sware unto thy fathers to give thee."

In this case the Israelites benefited from God's promises that they would experience a direct relationship between obedience and blessing.

Obedience to God would result in their numbers increasing, their crops and animal herds flourishing, and protection from diseases.

Deuteronomy 10:19-22 reads, "Love ye therefore the stranger: for ye were strangers in the land of Egypt. Thou shalt fear the Lord thy God; him shalt thou serve, and to him shalt thou cleave, and swear by his name. He is thy praise, and he is thy God, that hath done for thee these great and terrible things, which thine eyes have seen. Thy fathers went down into Egypt with threescore and ten persons; and now the Lord thy God hath made thee as the stars of heaven for multitude."

God requires us to love our fellow man. We are to fear God and show Him respect for who He is whenever possible. No day should pass without praising and thanking God for His continual love and many blessings.

Deuteronomy 11:26-27 reads, "Behold, I set before you this day, a blessing and a curse. A blessing, if ye obey the commandments of the Lord your God, which I command you this day: And a curse, if ye will not obey the commandments of the Lord your God, but turn aside out of the way which I command you this day, to go after other gods, which ye have not know."

It is repeated many times over that blessings are directly related to the obedience to God's commandments. Disobedience to God's commandments will be met with a curse that can have repercussions for generations. A major problem for man has always been other gods. Man can easily become obsessed with other interests that will prevent him from worshiping God. Man's fallen nature presents a continual struggle that will block spiritual growth and will cause conflict in areas that were once considered resolved.

Deuteronomy 28:1-8 reads, "And it shall come to pass, if thou shalt hearken diligently unto the voice of the Lord thy God, to observe and to do all his commandments which I command thee this day, that the Lord thy God will set thee on high above all nations of the earth. And all these blessings shall come on thee, and overtake thee, if thou salt hearken unto the voice of the Lord thy God. Blessed shall be the fruit of thy body, and fruit of thy ground, and the fruit of thy cattle, and increase of thy kine, and the flocks of thy sheep. Blessed shalt thou be when thou comest in, and blessed shalt thou be when thou goest out. The Lord shall cause thine enemies that rise up against thee to be smitten before thy face: they shall come out against thee one way, and flee before thee seven ways. The Lord shall command the blessing upon thee in thy in thy storehouses, and in all that thou settest thine hand unto; and he shall bless thee in the land which the Lord thy God giveth thee."

The blessings of obedience have a real impact on the daily life of those that are living each day in obedience to God's word. They have a daily prayer life that begins with thanksgiving for the many blessings they have received. We all experience countless blessings each day that we need to be aware of and thank God for these blessings. Unfortunately, many are lost in the race for wealth and until man comes to the realization that greed is a sin we will continue to experience a political system that is corrupt and lead by corrupt leaders. Our current society encourages and values individuals that hoard money and things. Many of these individuals have more money than they will ever need and have no social conscious for the poor and their neighbor.

God loved and blessed the Jewish people and was going to fulfill His covenant with them to deliver them to the promise land. Moses was the humblest man on earth who had many personal frailties. God was able to mold Moses into a great leader to be used to accomplish many great miracles and bless the Jewish people. Blessings came in many different forms. God provided direction, protection from the plagues, food and water in the desert, protection from enemy armies in Egypt and in the desert. God was with the Jewish people each day providing countless blessings. However, sin and disobedience was not tolerated and was met with God's discipline.

The relationship between God and the Israelites was in some respects similar to a parent-child relationship. However, our Lord is a sovereign, just, loving God that provides blessings in a dynamic way that can be accompanied by direction, discipline, and a demand for obedience. For example, God provided blessings on a daily basis for the Israelites for 40 years in many different ways. Even though God was faithful, the Israelites fell into idol worship when Moses did not return after a few weeks in the mountains. God's initial response was to destroy the Israelites. It was only after Moses pleaded, begged and prayed that God allowed the Israelites to live. Idol worship was not tolerated.

Many churches today speak of God's love and blessings. But, our understanding of God's sovereignty and power is limited. His message is clear and consistent; we need to love God with all our hearts, minds, and to love our neighbors. The worship of idols is a sin that easily evokes the wrath of God and in some ways is the most pervasive sin we see today. We are in a world that is obsessed with greed, the love of money, and possessions.

The believer's life is filled by the Holy Spirit and directed to love God with all of his heart, and show that love to his neighbor. His life is under the Holy Spirit's instruction in many different ways throughout life experiences and trials. Once a decision is made to believe that Jesus died for our sins a new journey begins. This journey involves walking down a path lead by the Holy Spirit in prayer. God will use events, other people, education, and many other life experiences to mold, build, and change believers with His unique plan for each believer.

As God guided and directed Moses and the Israelites so did Jesus guide and direct the disciples. In turn, Jesus left the Holy Spirit to guide and direct believers. The message is clear, God, Jesus, and the Holy Spirit provide guidance for the believer that includes obedience to His word and commandments. The Holy Spirit guides us today in a dynamic way in an ever-changing world.

Contentment is achieved at the point we realize our faith is mature and we rest completely in the loving arms of our Savior. God created each unique individual to fill a unique purpose in life.

APPLICATION

It is estimated that Moses led the Hebrew people out of Egypt about 1513 B.C. and that the Hebrew people lived in Egypt for about 430 years. It is believed that Ram was the leader of the tribe of Judah during this time period and was involved in the exodus. Leading hundreds of people through the desert would have been extremely difficult and meeting their daily needs would have been very demanding.

Very little is known about Ram and his life as a leader of the tribe of Judah. Leaving Egypt and escaping the backbreaking life of a slave would have brought great joy to all of the Hebrew people for a time. However, after spending some time in the desert and realizing how difficult life was with little food and water the Hebrew people quickly began to complain.

God heard the prayers of the Hebrew people and sent Moses and Aaron to force the Pharaoh of Egypt to release the Hebrew people from slavery. God through Moses sent ten plagues that destroyed the crops, animals, and delivered death to the first born of each Egyptian family. God also protected each Hebrew family from these plagues, destroyed the Pharaoh's army, and the death of the first born. God understood the plight of the Hebrew people and responded by providing a way to escape slavery and persecution. The Hebrew people were initially thankful and made sacrifices to their Lord God. However, that was short lived until they were faced with the realities of living in the desert and traveling through hostile lands. God did not leave them, but continued to guide them day and night, and provide them with food and water.

God was very loving, patience and concerned about the Hebrew people even when they were constantly complaining. However, those that complained against Moses and Aaron for their leadership did not live a long life. The Hebrew people were beaten for many years to the point where fear was in control of the entire generation. It is believed that Ram and the tribe of Judah was part of this generation and spent their lives in the wilderness. They prayed for forgiveness and made sacrifices and God gave them forgiveness.

Only a loving God full of grace would continually forgive a people that failed so many times in so many different situations. God's love for mankind is without end and He disciplines those who he loves so that they may be made complete. His patience is always present and is freely given to all those who ask for forgiveness. He is a personal God who will answer your prayers in a loving way and direct your paths as He directed the paths of the Hebrew people.

Amminadab and wife unknown
(Approx. 1453–unknown)

IT IS BELIEVED THAT the conquest of Canaan began about 1406 BC with Joshua being directed by God. It is also believed that spies were sent into Canaan about 1444 BC. Two of the spies, Joshua and Caleb, reported that the land could be captured and 10 other spies said the people were too strong to be captured. The Israelites refused to enter the land of Canaan. Because of their disobedience, God required the Israelites to spend the next 40 years wandering the desert.

Ruth 4:19 reads, "And Hezron begat Ram, and Ram begat Amminadab." Amminadab (meaning a people of liberty) was again believed to be a man of leadership within the tribe of Judah and in the lineage of Jesus. It is believed he was born in Egypt and probably died in the wilderness as a leader of the tribe of Judah.

It is believed that Amminadab was only a child during the exodus from Egypt and did spend most of his life with the Israelites wandering in the desert searching for freedom and the Promised Land.

It is recorded that Joshua (Approx. 1475 to 1365 BC) replaced Moses as the leader of the Israelites upon Moses death around 1407 BC. According to the Bible Joshua was born in Egypt and was an assistant to Moses for many years during the exodus from Egypt. He was also one of the twelve spies that traveled to Canaan to report on the condition of the land, strength of the people that lived in that area and if the cities were walled. Joshua and Caleb were the only two spies that provided a truthful assessment of the land, people and encouraged the invasion of Canaan. The other ten spies were fearful and lied about the strength of the people and the land. Again, we see another example of man's sin and God's discipline. In this case the

Israelites were forced to wander the wilderness for another 40 years until most of the existing generation over the age of 20 died.

The book of Joshua is placed in the canon as the first of twelve historical books (from Joshua to Esther) that follows the sequence of the Septuagint. The purpose of the book is to give an official account of the conquest of Canaan (the promised land) and the fulfillment of the Abrahamic covenant. God used Joshua to develop and lead a force that conquered Canaan and fulfilled the covenant He made with Abraham. The methods and military strategies used to complete this task were unique, directed by God and specifically designed to subdue a people that were totally immersed in the worship of idols and other pagan gods. For example, the walls of Jericho fell when Joshua's Israelite army marched around the city blowing their trumpets. At this point in time God was unfolding His plan for His people and completing the covenant He made with Abraham. Consequently, many pagan kings and all those involved in sinful acts were destroyed. Obviously, no person or sin will be allowed to prevent the unfolding of God's covenant or plans. Joshua was very successful during his life as a leader as long as he lived a life that was in obedience to God's word. As Joshua, we live out our lives in circumstances that at times feels like we are in a battle. Joshua's successes were dependent on his obedience to God's word as are our successes depend on being obedience to God's word. Regardless of the world and our circumstance we need to be prepared to meet our Creator.

The land of Canaan is a promised land that is like no other land in the world. God chose this land and its people to be priests of God's word. The requirement to dwell with God in this land was to be obedient to God's word and maintain a pure heart. We also need to remember to dwell with God you need to be always on guard and run from sin. Our only hope rests in the knowledge and assurance that our lives have been purified from sin by the death of God's only Son.

Joshua 8:33-34 reads, "And all Israel, and their elders, and officers, and their judges, stood on this side the ark and that side before the priests the Levites, which bare the ark of the covenant of the Lord, as well the stranger, as he that was born among them, half of them over against mount Grasim, and half of them over against mount Ebal; as Moses the servant of the Lord had commanded before, that they should bless the people of Israel. And afterward he read all the word of the law, the blessings and cursings, according to all that is written in the book of the law."

Before entering the Promised Land Joshua assembled all the Israelites and built an altar of uncut stones on Mount Ebal and made sacrifices of burnt offerings to God for the capture of the city of Ai and Jericho which were both involved in the worship of idols and pagan Gods. Joshua separated the twelve tribes and placed them on both Mount Ebal and Mount Gerizim. At mount Ebal the Levites shouted the list of curses on the people for disobedience that included, idolatry, dishonoring their father and mother, dishonesty, stealing, lying, immorality, and murder. The curses related to this disobedience were famine, disease, confusion, mental health issues, barrenness, loss of property, and death. It is believed 50,000 were exiled to other lands for disobedience. Disobedience to God's commands carries a severe penalty.

Galatians 3:13 reads, " Christ hath redeemed us from the curse of the law, being made a curse for us: for it is written, Cursed is every one that hangeth on a tree. That the blessing of Abraham might come on the Gentiles through Jesus Christ; that we might receive the promise of the Spirit through faith."

The death of God's only Son, Jesus Christ paid the price for all the sins of mankind. This single event allows all of mankind to spend eternity with their Creator if they believe the word of God and the ultimate sacrifice of His Son for the payment of all our sins. For man to build and maintain a relationship with His creator he must confess his sins and obey God's commandments. Sin is like a cancer that will grow and spread and affect every aspect of a person's life. Consequently, the identity and confession of sin on a daily basis is paramount for a Christian to grow and survive.

It has been said that confession is good for the soul. Man has many frailties and is vulnerable to many different types of sinful thoughts and acts. Changing a man's life and cleansing his soul begins with confession of all sin that includes sin filled thoughts and actions. Confession requires one to spend time identifying these sins and asking God for His forgiveness. This daily time in prayer allows God to strengthen our Christian life and develop a closer walk with our Lord and Savior.

1 John 1:9 reads, "If we confess our sins, he is faithful and just to forgive us our sins, and to cleanse us from all unrighteousness."

A Christian's heart's desire is to understand God's direction, to be in communion with his Creator, and to live a life that is pleasing to his Lord and Savior. God is the same yesterday, today, and forever. He is a loving, patience God that cannot and will not tolerate sin. It was only because of Moses' pleads and prayers that God did not destroy the Israelites after they molded the gold idol. The world today refuses to acknowledge God's creations and blessings just as the Israelites refused to worship God and returned to worshiping a golden calf. Man is trapped in the same vicious cycle of disobedience, God's discipline, confession and repentance, and God's blessings which has been repeated since the fall of man. The fall of man created a huge crevasse between God and man. Man had eaten from the tree of knowledge and was filled with pride and was confident he was able to resolve all issues that he would encounter. He felt he did not need God and was clever enough to plan for his own destiny and to survive any obstacle on this planet. Man refused to follow God's direction and trusted in his own devices to survive. Man created his own gods that resulted in a man that was selfish, greedy and desperately wicked in every thought.

The covenant God made to Abraham unfolded over hundreds of years and involved a series of events as the Jewish people traveled to the Promised Land. On the journey the Jewish people failed and became disobedient on many occasions for many reasons and in many different locations. God's love for His chosen people was always there listening to their prayers, blessing them and on occasion disciplining them. Their very survival was dependent of God's direction, protection and blessings.

Today, God has made a covenant with all of mankind. The terms of the covenant are simple and straight forward. All those who believe that God made the ultimate sacrifice of His only Son and obey His commandments will spend eternity in heaven.

The Israelites were caught in a continual spiral of disobedience and failures. In each case God disciplines them and later provided a blessing and a way to escape. In this situation the children of Israel disobeyed God's commands and were disciplined by God allowing them to fall under the rule of the Philistines. In turn, God provided them with Samson, a man blessed by God to grow to be a man of great strength and responsible for the defeat of many of Israel's enemies. Samson on one occasion killed a thousand Philistines with the jaw of an ass.

Judges 13:24 reads, "And the woman bare a son, and called his name Samson: and the child grew, and the Lord blessed him."

The birth of Samson was a blessing for the Israelites. However, the book of Judges includes another example of discipline and blessings. The Jewish people were disobedient to God's word and did not follow Moses or

Jacob's direction. The results were once again God's just reaction by allowing the Philistines to gain control over the Israelites.

Samson was blessed with great strength and able to defeat the Philistines and protect the Jewish people, but his disobedience to God's word and human frailties caused him great failures.

Our God is a sovereign and just Savior who loved and cared for the children of Israel. Unfortunately, the Jewish people once again failed with years of disobedience that was once again met with God's discipline with years of rule by the Philistines. Eventually after years of prayers and confession they were blessed with Samson a man that could provide them with protection.

In this case, blessings were experienced by Samson and all the children of Israel over a period of many years. In addition, Samson eventually failed and sinned in disobedience and lost his life. The importance of avoiding sin and being obedient to God's commandments cannot be stressed enough. A Christian's life is based on a strong communion with his Lord and Savior which is critical for God's plan to be developed and realized by the Christian. A Christian's life is focused on living a life to please God and to be prepared to meet his Creator. A Christian wants to hear the words "Well done my good and faithful servant." (Matt: 25:21).

APPLICATION

The Jewish people were slaves in Egypt for hundreds of years which made transitioning to freedom difficult in many ways. Under slavery they had developed ways of meeting their basic needs for water, food and shelter. However, in the wilderness they were faced with the reality that water, food and shelter would be difficult to find. They had gone from exultation of seeing their oppressors destroyed to the harsh realities of the desert and the lack of resources. A celebration of joy and praise sunk into bitter complaining and rebellion. The spies sent out by Moses returned with negative reports and lies about the dangers of the Promised Land. The Jewish people lost all faith in their God and fell into a deep depression. God determined that the Jewish people would need another 40 years before they would be prepared to conquer the Promised Land.

Our circumstances can at times be overwhelming and we feel at times lost. However, we need to remember that God is with us always even in the most difficult of times. God is with us in times of worry, in making difficult decisions, and in living a life that meets God desires.

2 Corinthians 4:18 reads, "While we look not at the things which are seen, but at the things which are not seen: for the things which are seen are temporal; but the things which are not seen are eternal."

It is estimated that the Israelites crossed over the Jordan River and into the Promised Land about 1406 BC. After the land of Canaan was conquered, the land was divided among the tribes except for the tribe of Levi. God gave the tribe of Levi the task of caring for the spiritual needs of all the tribes and was given special considerations from each tribe.

Nahshon and wife unknown
(Approx. 1383–unknown)

GOD TOLD MOSES TO take a count and include the names of the Hebrew people that were twenty years and older.

Number 1:1-3 reads, "And the Lord spake unto Moses in the wilderness of Sinai in the tabernacle of the congregation, on the first day of the second month, in the second year after they were come out of the land of Egypt, saying, take ye the sum of all the congregation of the children of Israel, after their families, by the house of the families, by the number of their names, every male by their polls. From twenty years old and upward, all that are able to go forth to war in Israel: thou and Aaron shall number them by their armies."

God's reaction to the Israelites refusing to enter the Promised Land was one of discipline and judgment. He used the census taken in the Sinai to establish a guideline as to who would enter the Promised Land. A complete generation of Hebrew people would have their life shortened because of their refusal to obey God's direction. The only exception to this rule was Joshua and Caleb.

Numbers 14:29 reads, "Your carcases shall fall in this wilderness; and all that were numbered of you, according to your whole number, from twenty years old and upward, which have murmured against me,"

It is believed that Nahshon was the leader of the tribe of Judah when the Jewish people were traveling from Sinai to Kadesh Barnea. It is believed that Amminadab would not have entered into the Promised Land, but his son, Nahshon and his grandson Salmon, may have received the blessing to enter the Promised Land.

Nahshon was chosen as captain of the children of Judah and one of the twelve chosen to be captain of the different tribes. The tribe of Judah was located on the east side of the tabernacle which was considered a place of honor.

Numbers 2:3 reads, "And on the east side toward the rising of the sun shall they of the standard of the camp of Judah pitch throughout their armies: and Nahshon the son of Amminadab shall be captain of the children of Judah."

Ruth 4:20 reads, "And Amminadah begat Nahshon, and Nahshon begat Salmon."

Nahshon was a leader and would follow the cloud of God by day and the pillar of fire by night. Nahahon was the son of Amminadab and the fifth generation of Judah. It is also believed that Nahahon lead and encouraged the tribe of Judah to struggle for freedom and at the same time maintained the lineage of Jesus.

It is believed Nahahon was living during the time of Joshua and would have been subject to his rule and involved in capturing the land of Canaan. As a leader Nahahon would have been aware that the purpose of a leader is to be a servant.

1 Peter 2:16 reads, "As free, and not using your liberty for a cloak of maliciousness, but as the servants of God."

APPLICATION

We must never glorify ourselves. God may select some to be leaders, but these positions are for the purpose of being servants. The life of a Christian is the life that is lived in humble faith. God recognizes this faith and covers that Christian with a blanket of grace. Joshua and Caleb were examples of a Christian living a life in humble faith.

James 4:6 reads, "But he giveth more grace. Wherefore he saith, God resisteth the proud, but giveth grace unto the humble."

Deuteronomy 31:7-9 reads, "And Moses called unto Joshua, and said unto him in the sight of all Israel, Be strong and of good courage: for thou must go with this people unto the land which the Lord hath sworn unto their fathers to give them; and thou shalt cause them to inherit it. And the Lord, he it is that doth go before thee; he will be with thee, he will not fail thee, neither be dismayed. And Moses wrote this law, and delivered it unto the priests the sons of Levi, which bare the ark of the covenant of the Lord, and unto all the elders of Israel."

Both Joshua and Caleb would enter the Promised Land with God's strength and guidance. It is the faith that lived within them that allowed God's grace to freely flow and bless them and protected them as they captured city after city and defeated many armies.

Christians need to realize that making a confession of faith is just the beginning. Just as Joshua and Caleb, Christians need to move forward with prayer in faith into the abundant life that God has prepared for them.

Salmon and Rachab
(Approx. 1333–1233)

RUTH 4:20 READS, "AND Amminadah begat Nahahon, and Nahahan begat Salmon."

Salmon was the great, great, grandfather of King David and was from the tribe of Judah. He was also living during the time of Joshua and would have been involved in the capturing of the land of Canaan the Promised Land. He was married to Rachab and had a son Boaz. Rachab was the woman who hid Joshua's two spies that were sent to collect information about the city of Jericho.

Joshua recognized Rachab for her willingness to risk her life to hide the spies and to assist the Israelites. Her life and the life of her family were spared because she listened to God's direction and was obedient to His will for her life. God took a woman that was completely involved in sin and gave her a godly husband and included her in the lineage of the Messiah, Jesus Christ.

We see in the Bible example after example of God using ordinary people to accomplish extraordinary tasks. Today we see ordinary people mired in sin trying to justify and promote their life style as acceptable and as part of society's norms. God can speak to any of these lost souls at any moment and change their lives as He changed Rachab's life.

Unfortunately, many of these lost souls are like Lot's wife. Lot's wife was a highly intelligent woman, a professor of religion and had access to Abraham. She loved Sodom and its people and their life style and could not walk away. Many are highly intelligent and well educated like Lot's wife and are completely addicted to their desires and cannot break away from a life that will only bring death.

APPLICATION

The Apostle of Paul tells us of the eternal and unchanging truth found in the Bible and the man's limited understanding of those truths.

1 Corinthians 2: 10-13 reads, "But God hath revealed them unto us by his Spirit: for the Spirit searcheth all things, yea, the deep things of God. For what man knoweth the things of a man, save the spirit of man which is in him? even so the things of God knoweth no man, but the spirit of God. Now we have received, not the spirit of the world, but the spirit which is of God; that we might know the things that are freely given to us of God. Which things also we speak, not in the words which man's wisdom teacheth, but which the Holy Ghost teacheth; comparing spiritual things with spiritual."

The Apostle Paul's mission was simply to communicate God's truth as found in the Bible. Only the Holy Ghost is able to teach spiritual truth to man. Man's ability to know and understand another man's thoughts is very limited if not impossible. It is only through the Holy Spirit that man is able to begin to understand spiritual truths.

The disobedience and rebellion by the Israelites for not entering the Promised Land resulted in hundreds of thousands of lives being cut short. Consequently, the importance of following God's direction for your life cannot be minimized.

It is believed that Salmon as leader of the tribe of Judah was young enough to enter the Promised Land and would have assisted Joshua and Caleb. Eventually Salmon married a woman by the name of Rachab, who was responsible for helping two of Joshua's spies that were trapped in the city of Jericho. God assisted these two spies by changing the heart of Rachab, a Canaanite.

Joshua 2:9-11 reads," And she said unto the men, I know that the Lord hath given you the land, and that your terror is fallen upon us, and that all the inhabitants of the land faint because of you. For we have heard how the Lord dried up the water of the Red Sea for you, when ye came out of Egypt; and what ye did unto the two kings of the Amorites, that were on the other side Jordan, Sihon and Og, whom ye utterly destroyed. And as soon as we had heard these things, our hearts did melt, neither did there remain more courage in any man, because of you: for the Lord your God, he is God in heaven above, and in earth beneath."

It was Rachab's faith that changed her life and the lives of many others. She lived the life of a prostitute, but God still selected her because of her heart and willingness to follow His direction. She acted on her faith in the

God of Israel which allowed the spies to escape and allowed God's plan to continue in the destruction of Jericho.

Salmon was one of the two spies that Rachab hid in her home. Their marriage placed Rachab in the royal genealogy of the Messiah, Jesus Christ. The other foreign ancestors in the genealogy of the Messiah are Tamar, Ruth and Bathsheba. It is God's grace that erases all sin and allows a new life to begin again in faith. Jesus Christ came and died on the cross to save sinners. He was born of sinners and knew of the sinner's life, but committed no sin.

Isaiah 1: 18 reads, "Come now, and let us reason together, saith the Lord: though your sins be as scarlet, they shall be as white as snow; though they be red like crimson, they shall be as wool."

The power of God changed Rachab from a great sinner to a believer and a follower of the true God. God revealed the depth of His mercy and was exalted. Our salvation is a free gift that can never be earned. When God's work is done we all stand together as believers praising and glorifying our Lord and Savior.

Boaz and Ruth
(Approx. 1273–1193 BC)

BOAZ WAS A WEALTHY land owner in Bethlehem in Judea and the son of Salmon and Rachab. He was also in the genealogy of the Messiah, Christ Jesus. Boaz learned of Naomi and Ruth and their many difficulties. Boaz provides food for them and intentionally left grain for them to collect. Boaz accepts Ruth's proposal and marries her and they have a son Obed. Obed continues the lineage of David's royal house and the Messiah, Jesus Christ by becoming the father of Jesse and the grandfather of David.

Again we see God accept a person outside the Israelite community a Gentile (Ruth was a Moabite) to eventually bring David into the world. Jesus is often referred to the "Son of David" and David is referred to as the "Son of Jesse".

APPLICATION

Naomi was destitute after the death of her husband and two sons. She traveled with her daughter-in-law Ruth from Moab to Judah to visit Boaz, a friend of Naomi's late husband, Elimelech. Ruth was a young woman that decided to stay with Naomi for the purpose of caring for her in collecting food and finding shelter.

Ruth gleaned the fields after the harvest by Boaz's workers, which was an appropriate Jewish custom. Boaz discovered who Ruth was and made arrangements for her protection and access to more food and drink.

Ruth was extremely grateful for Boaz's kindness and asked why he showed all this kindness toward her. He responded by telling her he knew of the kindness that she gave to Naomi and the death of her husband and the death of Naomi's husband. Boaz also offers a blessing to Ruth.

Ruth 2:12 reads, "The Lord recompense thy work, and a full reward be given thee of the lord God of Israel, under whose wings thou art come to trust."

Ruth responded and asked that Boaz protect her and provide provisions. According to Jewish custom this would be way of asking Boaz to take her as his wife.

God loves all of mankind and commands his people to show love and care for the poor. God's love was revealed through Boaz as he was merciful, compassionate, and kind to Ruth, a Moabite widow. That same love and compassion was shown by Ruth through her commitment to Naomi.

God used both Boaz and Ruth to further his royal bloodline for both the Jew and Gentile. Ruth would become the great grandmother of King David unfolding God's plan that Jesus would be the Son of David and Messiah for both the Jew and Gentile.

As Christians we need to be aware of how we view people and realize they are God's creation and He has a plan for their lives. God's plan for their life may include meeting responsible Christians that are willing to share their faith and the experience of living a God directed life. Ruth was an outsider, a poor Gentile who would have had no place in this land Judah. However, Boaz viewed Ruth as a compassionate, loving person that was willing to dedicate her life to the care of Naomi and the worship of the true God of Israel.

Obed and wife unknown
(Approx. 1203–1123)

RUTH IMMIGRATED TO BETHLEHEM with her mother-in-law Naomi. Ruth married Boaz and they had a son Obed. Obed was the father of Jesse and the grandfather of David which was included in the lineage of the Messiah, Jesus Christ.

This time period would include the time of the judges from approximately 1254 BC to 1104 BC. This would also include the time between the death of Joshua and the appointment of Israel's first king, Saul. The death of Joshua brought about a new independent life for the Israelites and the opportunity to appoint judges for the purpose of making decisions. The fifteen judges that served during this time period would be considered to be recipients of divine grace and allowed to rule almost like kings.

The author of the book of Ruth (Approx. 1010 BC) is not known. Some believe it may have been Samuel.

Both Ruth and Naomi lost their husbands and both were under Jewish law that allowed them to gleam the fields after the harvest. These women were able to protect each other and God provided protection for both these widows. Boaz was a wealthy land owner who followed God's commandments and all Jewish rule. The consequence of following God's commands was that he was viewed as honest, considerate, and held in high esteem by all. In this case, employees of Boaz were asking for God to bless Boaz and keep him in good health.

Ruth 2:4 reads, "And, behold, Boaz came from Bethlehem, and said unto his reapers, The Lord be with you. And they answered him, The Lord bless thee."

At the time of Boaz, the poor were completely dependent on the landowners not to harvest all the crops, but leave some for the poor to collect.

Naomi and Ruth were two women who were dependent on Boaz and his generosity. As Christians we are dependent on each other for protection and generosity.

God blessed man with the ability to solve many problems. Man could work together to resolve the problems of world hunger, he could work together with others to resolve world conflicts, and he could resolve the problems of racial division. All of these issues are related to the heart and loving your neighbor as yourself. Namoi and Ruth loved each other and cared for each other in a time of need. And, because of this loving relationship they were blessed and survived.

Ruth 3:10 reads, "And he said, Blessed be thou of the Lord, my daughter: for thou hast showed more kindness in the latter end than at the beginning, inasmuch as thou followedst not young men, whether poor or rich."

Boaz was a man of honor, integrity and was sensitive to Ruth and her plight in life. He blessed her and praised her for her bold proposal. Boaz took additional steps to ensure the people of Bethlehem considered her to be a person of great reputation. God blessed man with the breath of life that gave man a soul capable of discerning good from evil. God also blessed man with emotions that are capable of experiencing love, hate, and the ability to express those emotions. Some of man's greatest blessings are experienced from music and the voices that sing praises to God for His great faithfulness in providing blessing after blessing.

Ruth 4:17 reads, "And the women her neighbors gave it a name, saying, there is a son born to Naomi; and they called his name Obed: he is the father of Jesse, the father of David."

Naomi's daughter-in-law Ruth was a great blessing to Naomi. Boaz married Ruth and bore a son, Obed. God's plan and blessings involved a man named Boaz and Ruth to be in a line of descendants that gave birth to King David, through whom our Savior the Lord Jesus Christ was born. These people were selected by God because of their willingness to be obedient to God's word and to be open to His plan and direction.

Ruth 4:21-22 reads, "And Salmon begat Boaz, and Boaz begat Obed, And Obed begat Jesse, and Jesse begat David."

Saul was the first King of Israel (Approx. 1080 -1012 BC). His rule experienced the same stages as other patriarchs. Saul was blessed by God, but failed to follow God commands and experienced God's discipline.

APPLICATION

Today, we also experience these same stages as we live out our lives. We are blessed in many ways today, but we also sin against God in many ways. For example, a person who steals has sinned against God for not trusting Him to provide for that need. A person that covets another person's possessions has sinned against God for not being grateful for those things God has provided. It is extremely important to thank God for each blessing and to praise and honor His name whenever possible. Today, following God's direction requires us to not only recognize God's directions, but to act on them and trust in His love and His wisdom.

Living a Christian life is a very loving and at the same time a pragmatic experience that requires our entire being to praise and honor our sovereign Lord and Savior at all times and in all situations. We need to remember our Lord and Savior cannot and will not tolerate sin. Consequently, man's only hope of salvation was for our loving God to make the ultimate sacrifice of offering the life of His only Son.

God used Ruth and Boaz in ways that would be impossible for us to foresee. With that in mind we need to be open to new avenues and people that God brings into our lives. God's love for mankind is without limits and looks at man's heart and how he may be used in God's plan. Man's outward appearance is not a consideration. God loves His creation and He demands love from those He created. Those that love God obey His commandments and show His love to others.

We receive love and blessing from God and blessings and love from others.

Ruth 4:11-12 reads, "And all the people that were in the gate, and the elders, said, We are witnesses. The Lord make the woman that is come into thane house like Rachel and like Leah, which two did build the house of Israel: and do thou worthily in Ephratah, and be famous in Bethlehem: And let thy house be like the house of Pharez, whom Tamar bare unto Judah, of the seed which the Lord shall give thee of this young woman."

The people of Bethlehem and the elders gathered at the gate of Boaz's house and blessed both Ruth and Boaz and their marriage. The people of Bethlehem also blessed Naomi, Ruth and Boaz when Ruth gave birth to Obed. There was great joy in Bethlehem when this union was made and Obed would continue the bloodline.

Asking for God's blessing on another Christian is extremely important and needs to be a common practice in our churches today. It is a practice that has fallen to the side with so many pressing issues in today's culture. The prayers of a righteous man can have a profound effect on a fellow Christian's life. These prayers should be sought after and cherished for their power to change lives.

James 5:16 reads, "Confess your faults one to another, and pray one for another, that ye may be healed. The effectual fervent prayer of a righteous man availeth much."

The prayers that are made to our Lord are able to heal the sick, bring joy to a person lost in grief, and rebuild lives that have been destroyed. As a Christian, our priorities change from being focused on self to being focused on others.

Ephesians 4:29 reads, "Let no corrupt communication proceed out of your mouth, but that which is good to the use of edifying, that it may minister grace unto the heavens."

Obed was blessed with many prayers and fulfilled the bloodline and the prophecies that a Messiah would come from the tribe of Judah and be a Son of David. Blessings from God will provide good health, a good harvest, and release future blessings. It is important that prayers for blessings are made daily for the protection of the entire family, for healthy bodies, and opportunities to share God's message of love.

Jesse and wife unknown
(Approx. 1140–1020 BC)

GOD SENT THE PROPHET Samuel to the home of Jesse to anoint the next King of Israel. The prophet Samuel under God's direction interviewed all of Jesse's eight sons from the tribe of Judah. David the youngest son was selected by God because of his heart.

1 Samuel 16:7 reads, "But the Lord said unto Samuel, Look not in his countenance, or on the height of his stature; because I have refused him: for man looketh on the outward appearance, but the Lord looketh on the heart."

David was eventually appointed king over Judah and later king over Israel. God was using Samuel to determine David's heart, spirit, and soul. David loved God and took delight in pleasing and obeying God's word. The heart will determine how one believes and the mouth will confess that faith that is needed to be saved for all eternity. The mouth is used to confess faith to please God and not man.

The prophet Isaiah in about 740 BC prophesied that the Messiah, Jesus Christ would be a descendant of the family of Jesse and of the tribe of Judah. A few years later the northern kingdom of Israel would fall captive to the Assyrian monarchs and the Israelites were exiled to foreign lands. The land of Judah would also fall captive and the people exiled. Many years later the Assyrian empire was overthrown by Babylon which plundered Jerusalem and its temple. The exiled Jewish people were allowed to return to Israel and Jerusalem in about 537 BC.

Isaiah 11: 1-3 reads, "And there shall come forth a rod out of the stem of Jesse, and a branch shall grow out of his roots: And the spirit of the Lord shall rest upon him, the spirit of wisdom and understanding, the spirit of counsel and might, the spirit of knowledge and of the fear of the Lord. And shall make him of quick understanding in the fear of the Lord: and he shall not judge after the sight of his eyes, neither reprove after the hearing of his ears:"

Life was coming out of the family of Jesse and out of the tribe Judah. This new life was coming from the family of Jesse and his son David through which the Messiah would be born. The Spirit of the Lord came upon David when he was anointed King and would rest upon David's descendants. The Holy Spirit would bring upon David and his descendants (the Messiah, Jesus Christ) the knowledge and the fear of the Lord, the spirit of understanding and council, and the ability to rule justly.

God had warned Israel going all the way back to Moses that they would face judgment.

2 Kings 17:13 reads, "Yet the Lord testified against Israel, and against Judah, by all the prophets, and by all seers, saying, Turn ye from your evil ways, and keep my commandments and my statutes, according to all the law which I commanded your fathers, and which I sent to you by my servants the prophets."

The defeat and exile of the Jewish people from Israel and Judah was because the Jewish people sinned against God. We see example after example of the Jewish people sinning and then having to suffer the consequences.

Hebrews 12:7 reads, "If ye endure chastening, God dealeth with you as with sons; for what son is he whom the father chasteneth not?"

The faithful son is disciplined in divine love as in the glory with many sons.

The Lord spoke to Samuel the Prophet (Approx. 1120 -971 BC) at an early age and told him of the destruction of the house of Eli. Many learned of Samuel's encounter and he was eventually established as a prophet of the Lord. This is an example of God taking a poor servant and transforming him into a great Prophet.

Samuel was known as a great prophet and provided the Israelites with direction in defeating the Philistines and pushing the tribe out of the land. This resulted in many years of peace. During this time Samuel had two sons who he appointed as his successors. However, they were both rejected by the Israelites as unworthy. God controlled who was to lead his people and would often reject family successors. God at this point in time allowed Samuel to meet Saul. It became obvious to Samuel that Saul should be the next king. Saul did not follow Samuel's direction in defeating the Amalekites and was later removed as king. Samuel then traveled to Bethelehem where he anointed David as king.

1 Samuel 16:13 reads, "Then Samuel took the horn of oil, and anointed him in the midst of his brethren: and the Spirit of the Lord came upon David from that day forward. So Samuel rose up, and went to Ramah."

The prophet Samuel found David in a field as a shepherd. David was the youngest of eight children whose father was Jesse from the tribe of Judah. David's first encounter with Saul was when he was asked to perform before the king as a musician. David was also successful as a warrior when he challenged the Philistine giant Goliath with a sling and a stone. This was another example of God selecting a man from humble beginnings and molding him into a great leader. David's popularity grew quickly among the people and he was eventually appointed king of Judah. At this point in time the kingdoms of Judah and Israel were in conflict. Eventually, David was able to unite the two kingdoms and became the king.

APPLICATION

Boaz and Ruth had a son named Obed and his son was named Jesse. Jesse was a farmer who lived in Bethlehem and was from the tribe of Judah. Jesse had eight sons with David being the youngest. God sent Samuel the prophet to Bethlehem and to Jesse's home to anoint the next king. Jewish tradition dictates that the first born child would receive the family blessings.

At this point, God intervenes and instructs Samuel as to who would be anointed as the next king. Jesse presents seven of his sons to Samuel as candidates for anointment, but all were rejected by God because of their hearts. They all appeared to be excellent candidates from an outward appearance, but their hearts were not suitable to be king. Finally, Samuel discovers David the youngest brother out in the field tending sheep and God decides to anoint David as king.

Today's society evaluates men from their outward appearance and their accomplishments. In other words, God is not looking at man's height, weight, nationality, accomplishments, or wealth. He is focused on man's heart. A heart of God is a heart that is able to love unconditionally and freely forgive the unforgiveable. The power of the Holy Spirit indwells and communes with man's spirit and soul and allows man to change his anger to love.

Psalm 62:8 reads, "Trust in him at all times; ye people, pour out your heart before him: God is a refuge for us. Selah."

God is the source for safety, the deliverances from harm, and salvation for all. We need to set our priorities to first ask for God's blessings in our daily lives. We do not completely understand the scope and meaning of God's blessings. We use the word blessings frequently without understanding the full impact of God's blessings.

It is important that we realize we need to ask for His blessings in our daily lives. The reason being, that God's blessings protects us from countless difficulties seen and unseen. God's blessings can prevent disease from occurring in our bodies, guide us in ways to avoid danger, and open His path for our lives. In other words, it is paramount that we begin each day thanking God for His many blessings and asking for His blessings to be poured out upon our lives. The world and its millions of people presents many of the dangers that we encounter on a daily basis.

Protection and security from these dangers begins with finding and receiving God's grace and favor. However, finding and receiving God's favor and grace does not mean you will not experience hardships. Moses, Noah and countless other righteous men had to struggle with difficulties as they were molded, instructed and failed to obey God's commands.

As we humble our hearts before God, the Holy Spirit begins to reveal God's blessings that were otherwise taken for granted. The Holy Spirit is the great Comforter that puts the soul and the spirit at peace in knowing all is well. Our focus changes from self to others and what God has done in our lives. Appreciation and thankfulness has been lost in a society where entitlement has taken control of many minds.

It is extremely important that we are grateful for all of God's blessings and spend time each day thanking God for all he has done for us. Being ungrateful for God's blessings is a sin and will result in dire consequences.

Luke 17:11-19 reads, "And as he entered into a certain village, there met him ten men that were lepers, which stood afar off: And they lifted up their voices, and said, Jesus, Master, have mercy on us. And when he saw them, he said unto them, Go show yourselves unto the priests. And it came to pass, that, as they went, they were cleansed. And one of them, when he saw that he was healed, turned back, and with a loud voice glorified God. And fell down on his face at his feet, giving him thanks: and he was a Samaritan. And Jesus answering said, Were there not ten cleansed? but where are the nine? There are not found that returned to give glory to God, save this stranger. And he said unto him, Arise go thy way: thy faith hath made thee whole."

The Samaritan (a Gentile) was the only one that laid face down at Jesus' feet giving thanks. This was the only way to ensure God's blessing would be complete and salvation would take place. The Gentile was the only one who recognized Jesus as his Lord and Savior and received salvation. The only appropriate way to give thanks to God is to get down on our knees and pray a prayer of thanksgiving for each of the blessings He has given you. Developing a relationship with God requires one to first gain an appreciation of what He has done for you.

Moses, the Israelites, many others were disciplined many times for their sins. In other words, there is a direct relationship between sin and discipline. There is also a direct relationship between blessings and giving thanks for all of God's blessings. God's blessings are made complete in a sinner's life when thanks are given and accepted by God. There is also a direct relationship between gratitude and joy. As gratitude increases so does joy. Unfortunately, man's fallen nature only allows joy to last for a short period of time. For example, the joy of receiving additional money quickly fads as it replaced with the desire for more money. Joy can also be short lived when confronted by worry, fear, and depression.

God created man with a wide range of emotions that are appropriate in number of different situations.

Ecclesiastes 3:4 reads, "A time to weep, and a time to laugh; a timer to mourn, and a time to dance:"

However, a true lasting joy is possible when a relationship is developed between the sinner and His Creator. The knowledge of knowing God is in control and that our future is written in the lamb's book of life gives a peace and joy that goes beyond our understanding.

John 15:11 reads, "These things have I spoken unto you, that my joy might remain in you, and that your joy might be full."

David and Bathsheba
(Approx. 1040–970BC)

IT WAS THE GRACE of God that selected David to be chosen. David realized and understood this relationship was due to God's grace and nothing he could achieve. He loved God with all his heart and soul and strived to be obedient in all ways. Psalms 89: 3-4 reads, "I have made a covenant with my chosen, I have sworn unto David my servant, Thy seed will I establish forever, and build up thy throne to all generations. Selah." God blessed David in many ways and allowed him to defeat many armies, plan the building of the temple, write the book of Psalms, kill Goliath, and much more.

God spoke directly to David and God answered him.

1 Samuel 23:2-4 reads, "Therefore David inquired of the Lord, saying, Shall I go and smite these Philistines? And the Lord said unto David, Go, and smite the Philistines, and save Keilah. And David's men said unto him, Behold, we be afraid here in Judah: how much more than if we come to Keilah against the armies of the Philistines? Then David inquired of the Lord yet again. And the Lord answered him and said, Arise go down to Keilah; for I will deliver the Philistines into thine hand."

God answers David's question by providing directions and telling David He would deliver the Philistines to be defeated in battle. David was in direct contact with God and He provided David with tremendous confidence that allowed him to be a great leader for his army.

However, David was a fallen man, who fell short on many occasions with his affair with Bathsheba as one of the most egregious. David paid a heavy price for his sin with the loss of three of his sons, Amnon, Absalom, and Adonijah. His wives were also humiliated before all of Israel. Again, we see that it is only God's grace that allowed David to experience and understand the consequences of his sin. We serve a sovereign and just God that continues to remind us that disobedience will bring misery and death to those who continue to live a life that is focused on sin.

2 Samuel 7:4-8 reads, "And it, came to pass that night, that the word of the Lord came unto Nathan, saying, Go and tell my servant David, Thus saith the Lord, Shalt thou build me a house for me to dwell in? Whereas I have not dwelt in any house since the time that I brought up the children of Israel out of Egypt, even to this day, but have walked in a tent and in a tabernacle."

2 Samuel 7:12-17 reads, "And when thy days be fulfilled, and thou shalt sleep with thy fathers, I will set up thy seed after thee, which shall proceed out of thy bowels, and I will establish his kingdom. He shall build a house for my name, and I will establish the throne of his kingdom for ever. I shall be my son. If he commit iniquity, I will chasten him with the rod of men, and with the stripes of the children of men. But my mercy shall not depart away from him, as I took it from Saul, whom I put away before thee. And thine house and thy kingdom shall be established for ever before thee: thy throne shall be established for ever. According to all these words, and according to all this vision, so did Nathan speak unto David."

God made an unconditional promise to David that man's destiny would be established through David's bloodline. David would have a son (Solomon) who would also be king and continue to unfold God's plan to build a temple for the Ark of the Covenant. God is also reaffirming the promise of land He made in the Abrahamic and Mosaic covenants. This promise to David would further unfold into the everlasting blessing of the birth of another son and that son would be the Son of God the Messiah.

Both David and his son Solomon were blessed and were allowed to build a great kingdom for Israel. However, God allowed both of these men to make decisions that were not in keeping with either Jewish law or God's commandments. Both of these men disobeyed God's commandments and suffered the consequences.

Ecclesiastes 12:14 reads, "For God shall bring every work into judgment, with every secret thing, whether it be good, or whether it be evil."

1 Corinthians 3:13-15 reads, "Every man's work shall be made manifest: for the day shall declare it, because it shall revealed by fire; and the fire shall try every man's work of what sort it is. If any man's work abide which he hath built thereupon, he shall receive a reward. If any man's work shall be burned, he shall suffer loss: but he himself shall be saved; yet so as by fire."

All men will experience the absolute righteous judgment of God. Every believer will appear before the seat of Christ and have their lives evaluated to determine how they have used their God given talents. They may or may not receive a reward. However, all believers will be saved.

All men are to live a life that glorifies God, that is submissive to God's word, and to realize that all men will experience a divine judgment. The sacrifice of God's only Son allows all believers to spend eternity in heaven. However, all men will go through a divine judgment and some have built up great treasures in heaven from living a life that has honored God.

God blessed David in many ways for many years and used David to unfold His plan for the Jewish people. God protected David from his enemies and assisted him in capturing new land that expanded Israel's borders from the Mediterranean Sea to east of the Jordan River. During these many years God always allowed David to use his free will. Unfortunately, David made many bad decisions and disobeyed many of God's commands. David did understand the gravity of his mistakes and asked for God's forgiveness.

2 Samuel 7:25-28 reads, "And now, O Lord God, the word that thou hast spoken concerning thy servant, and concerning his house, establish it forever, and do as thou hast said. And let thy name be magnified for ever, saying, The Lord of hosts is the God over Israel: and let the house of thy servant David be established before thee. For thou, O Lord of host, God of Israel, hast revealed to thy servant, saying, I will build thee a house: therefore hath thy servant found in his heart to pray this prayer unto thee. And now, O Lord God, thou art that God, and thy words be true, and thou hast promised this goodness unto thy servant:"

2 Samuel 12:13 reads, "And David said unto Nathan, I have sinned against the Lord. And Nathan said unto David, The lord also hath put away thy sin; thou shalt not die."

David realized that God is our Creator and that He has asked us to love Him and our neighbor. He has created us with free will that allows us to make decisions for good or evil and to use our emotions to either love or hate. These decisions are ours to make and as we make more decisions as Christians we grow in love with our Lord and Savior. As we grow in trust and obey His commands we develop and experience God's love and the love for others.

Our God is a sovereign and just God that cannot tolerate sin. Consequently, we need to confess our sins each day to prevent separation from God and His blessings. Unfortunately, many are caught in sinful relationships and refuse to make a decision to move on even after being convicted by God's Spirit. John 8:11 reads, "She said, No man, Lord. And Jesus said unto her, Neither do I condemn thee: go and sin no more." Only God can make a judgment. However, we are to remove ourselves from sin and live a life that is pleasing to our Lord and Savior. God sacrificed His only Son for all the sins of man. There are no exceptions, we have all sinned and are subject to God's commandments.

David knew that confession was extremely important and that he needed to acknowledge his sin and asked for God's forgiveness. As it has been said, confession is good for the soul by reminding us of our sins and importance of taking corrective steps. Man is continually seeking to be sanctified and to cleanse his soul of sin.

Psalm 119:26 reads, "I have declared my ways, and thou heardest me: teach me thy statutes."

David was loved greatly by God for many reasons. David loved God's perfect word and spent many days writing and meditating on God word. It is believed that David was the author of over 70 psalms. Psalm 119: 47-48 reads, "And I will delight myself in thy commandments, which I have loved. My hands also will I lift up unto the commandments, which I have loved; and I will meditate in thy statutes." God did bless David with wisdom and understanding as he spent his days meditating on God's word.

David was also a man that praised and thanked God at every opportunity for all of his blessings. We should not let any day pass without thanking God for the continual flood of blessings. Psalm 100:4 reads, "Enter into his gates with thanksgiving, and into his courts with praise: be thankful unto him, and bless his name." Regardless of the situation, David thanked God for all of his blessings.

David realized he was not deserving of all his blessings and appealed to God's loving grace to forgive his many sins. We need to focus our attention on the undeserved, unfailing loving grace of a sovereign all powerful God.

David wanted to build a house for his Lord and God, but soon discovered that God wanted to build a house for David. This was more than just a royal temple, but a covenant between David and God where a kingdom was established where the Son of David would reign forever.

2 Samuel 7:11-14 reads, "And as since the time that I commanded judges to be over my people Israel, and have caused thee to reset from all thine enemies. Also the Lord telleth thee that he will make thee a house.

And when thy days be fulfilled, and thou shalt sleep with thy fathers, I will set up thy seed after thee, which shall proceed out of thy bowels, and I will establish his kingdom. He shall build a house for my name, and I will establish the throne of his kingdom for ever. I will be his father, and he shall be my son. If he commit iniquity, I will chasten him with the rod of men, and with the stripes of the children of men."

God made a covenant with David that he would build a house that would last forever. God and his Son (the Messiah) would build a house that would establish David's kingdom forever. God would raise His children as a father would raise his children with discipline if the child is disobedient.

It is believed that at this point the genealogy is different between Mary and Joseph. It is believed that Joseph was a descendant of Solomon one of King David's sons and Mary was the descendent of Nathan another one of King David's sons. Due to the traditional teachings of the Bible and the Gospel of Matthew the male genealogy will be followed from this point forward.

APPLICATION

All men want to experience joy, happiness, and peace in their lives. God's joy is available to all and will last forever in His creation.

Psalm 16:11 reads, "Thou will show me the path of life: in the presence is fullness of joy; at thy right hand there are pleasures for evermore."

Acts 13:52 reads, "And the disciples were filled with joy, and with the Holy Ghost."

John 16:24 reads, "Hitherto have ye asked nothing in my name: ask, and ye shall receive, that your joy may be full."

God created a world and a universe that holds and displays great beauty for all of mankind to enjoy and treasure. A Christian's joy is made complete with having the Holy Spirit enter into his life and commune with his spirit and soul. For man to experience the joy given by the Holy Spirit he must begin by humbly turning control of his life to God.

2 Samuel 6:14-16 reads, "And David danced before the Lord with all his might; and David was girded with a linen ephod. So David and all the house of Israel brought up the ark of the Lord with shouting, and with the sound of the trumpet."

John 15:11 reads, "These things have I spoken unto you, that my joy might remain in you, and that your joy might be full."

David knew he found favor with God when he brought the ark from the house of Obed-edom to Jerusalem. The joy of finding favor with God overtook David and he took off his kingly robe and began to dance, sing, and praise God. David's dance was never without thought of complete respect, reverence, honor, and glory for God. David's heart communed with God and the result was a soul that could not be kept captive. This rapture of the soul overflowed and could not be controlled by David as he lifted up his voice in praise of the presence of God's joy that was more then he could express. The joy of knowing God, His Son and experiencing the peace of the Holy Spirit is beyond measure and impossible to comprehend.

Like David, we all have sinned and have asked for forgiveness. This forgiveness was only possible with God's sacrifice of His only Son. This was a sacrifice that is beyond our comprehension and impossible for us to fully appreciate. Only in heaven will we fully realize this unbelievable gift and gain a full appreciation of all that God has done for each one of us.

Solomon and Naamah
Approximately (990–931 BC)

SOLOMON (APPROX. 970 TO 931 BCE) was born in Jerusalem as a child of David and Bathsheba. It is also believed that Solomon wrote the book of Proverbs as a way to share his wisdom in honoring and following God's commands. He also wrote the book Song of Solomon to show the joy of love and marriage from God. It is believed that it was God that convinced David to appoint Solomon as king.

1 Kings 2:45 reads, "And King Solomon shall be blessed, and the throne of David shall be established before the Lord for ever".

Solomon was raised in the house of David and was instructed by his father. He was well versed in the laws, rules and commandments of Moses. As the King, Solomon reviewed all those that held positions within the government and dismissed all those that were enemies to his success. Solomon was able to build a great army and a strong defense against invading tribes. He also strengthened trade agreements with other countries and kingdoms. It was his business savvy that lead him and Israel to become a very wealthy country that was envied by many of the surrounding kingdoms. Solomon as a fallen man had many faults that lead him to sin against God in many ways. These sins did not go unnoticed and eventually Solomon did pay for these sins with the loss of his rule as King.

Solomon was most famous for being blessed by God with great wisdom.

1 kings 3:5-10 reads, "In Gibeon the Lord appeared to Solomon in a dream by night: and God said, Ask what I shall give thee. And Solomon said, Thou hast showed unto thy servant David my father great mercy, according as he walked before thee in truth, and in righteousness, and in uprightness of heart with thee; and thou hast kept for him this great kindness, that hast

given him a son to sit on his throne, as it is this day. And now, O Lord my God, thou hast made thy servant king instead of David my father: and I am but a little child: I know not how to go out or come in. And thy servant is in the midst of thy people which thou hast chosen, a great people, that cannot be numbered nor counted for multitude. Give therefore thy servant an understanding heart to judge thy people, that I may discern between good and bad: for who is able to judge this thy so great a people? And the speech pleased the Lord, that Solomon had asked this thing."

Solomon did not ask for great wealth, possessions, a great army or many servants. He simply asked for wisdom and the ability to understand issues and to make the appropriate judgment. This simple request found favor with God and He blessed Solomon with great wisdom. Again, God made free will available and Solomon was allowed to make his own decisions regardless of the consequences.

God allowed Solomon to build the great temple to God in Jerusalem that was planned by David.

Even though Solomon was well versed in all of God's commandments he fell short in many different areas. In his later years He forgot about his devotion to God and allowed his wives to influence his worship of other gods.

It is believed that Solomon also wrote the book of Ecclesiastes.

Ecclesiastes 2:8-11 reads, "I gathered me also silver and gold, and the peculiar treasures of kings and of the peculiar treasury of kings and of the provinces: I gat me men singers and women singers, and the delights of the sons of men, as musical instruments, and that of all sorts. So I was great, and increased more than all that were before me in Jerusalem: also my wisdom remained with me. And whatsoever mine eyes desired I kept not from them. I withheld not my heart from any joy; for my heart rejoiced in all my labor: and this was my portion of all my labor. Then I looked on all the works that my hands had wrought, and on the labor that I had labored to do: and behold all was vanity and vexation of spirit, and there was no profit under sun".

Solomon realized after achieving great accomplishments that they were pale in comparison to God's love and plan for all of mankind. Man is to live by faith and to give God all the praise and glory and will never understand the mind of God. God chose Solomon to be part of His plan to unfold God's purpose. God blessed Solomon with great wisdom for God's purpose and only for God's purpose. Time is short for mankind and opportunities for building rewards are limited.

It is God's love that has allowed all men to make a decision between good and evil. It is that God given free will that creates an experience where man is able to freely love God without influence. Man can chose to live a life of good and follow God's commandments or live a life of sin and evil. God has always allowed sinful man the opportunity to make a decision to follow Him and His commandments.

King Solomon's sin eventually results in the separation of Israel into two countries (Israel and Judah) that were dominated by many different kings and occupied by foreign countries.

King Solomon was the second child born to King David and Bathsheba and would be included in the lineage for Joseph the father of the Messiah (Jesus Christ). Solomon had three brothers Nathan, Shammua, and Shobab. It is believed that Nathan was included in the lineage of Mary the mother of Jesus. Therefore, Jesus would be the Son of David from both Joseph and Mary's bloodlines. It is believed that Solomon married Naamah (an Ammonite and Gentile) and had a son Rehoboam.

King Solomon would be the first builder of the Temple and would fulfill David's dream to build a temple dedicated to Yahweh. He is also remembered as man of great wisdom, wealth, power, and a King who sinned. This sin was responsible for the splitting of Israel into two kingdoms, the northern Kingdom of Israel and the southern Kingdom of Judah. Solomon is also believed to be the author of the following books: "The Book of Proverbs", "The Book of Ecclesiastes", and "The Song of Solomon".

God blessed King Solomon greatly because he understood what was important in his life and the lives of those he lead.

1 Kings 3:9–12 reads, "Give therefore thy servant an understanding heart to judge thy people, that I may discern between good and bad: for who is able to judge this thy so great a people? And the speech pleased the Lord, that Solomon had asked this thing. And God said unto him, Because thou hast asked this thing, and hast not asked for thyself long life; nether hast asked riches for thyself, nor hast asked the life of thine enemies; but hast asked for thyself understanding to discern judgment; Behold, I have done according to thy words: lo, I have given thee a wise and understanding heart; so that there was none like thee before thee, neither after thee shall any arise like unto thee."

King Solomon placed the needs of God's people above his own needs and desires. God recognized Solomon had a servant's heart and would be responsive and obedient to God's direction. As long as Solomon remained faithful to the will of God he would be blessed and grow closer to his Lord.

It should be noted that King David provided Solomon with great insight as to how to prosper and succeed as a King and leader of God's people.

1 Kings 2:1-3 reads, "Now the day of David drew night that he should die; and he charged Solomon his son, saying, I go the way of all the earth: be thou strong therefore, and show thyself a man; And keep the charge of the Lord thy God, to walk in his ways, to keep his statutes, and his commandments, and his judgments, and his testimonies, as it is written in the law of Moses, that thou mayest prosper in all that thou doest, and whithersoever thou turnest thyself."

David was clear in his charge to Solomon that his success as a King would be dependent on his obedience and the obedience of God's people. God was going to bless Solomon and his rule if he was obedient to the laws of Moses. The same holds true today. God will bless and direct the path of those that follow God's commandments. God made a covenant with David that obedience to God's commandments would result in God establishing a kingdom from the seed of David that would last forever. This kingdom would be established on the birth, life, death, and resurrection of God's only Son, Jesus Christ.

Solomon at the end of his rule married foreign women and fell under their influence by worshiping pagan gods. This angered God and caused Him to allow Solomon's kingdom to disintegrate during Rahoboam's rule.

APPLICATION

God determined that Solomon would carry the Messiah's bloodline forward after David.

1 Chronicles 22:9 reads, "Behold a son shall be born to thee, who shall be a man of rest; and I will give him rest from all his enemies round about: for his name shall be Solomon, and I will give peace and quietness unto Israel in his days."

Solomon was a brilliant leader and under his leadership was able to build an extremely strong army and fortifications that brought about peace to Israel for many years. His gift of wisdom resulted in building a splendid temple in Jerusalem that was revered by all in the Mediterranean area. His management skills organized the monarchy and allowed it to function effectively and meet the needs of the people.

Solomon was a great man of prayer and would ask for blessings for all of the people of Israel.

1 Kings 8:55-61 reads, "And he stood, and blessed all the congregation of Israel with aloud voice, saying, Blessed be the Lord, that hath given rest unto his people Israel, according to all that he promised: there hath not failed one word of all his good promise, which he promised by the hand of Moses his servant. The Lord our God be with us, as he was with our fathers: let him not leave us, nor forsake us: That he may incline our hearts unto him, to walk in all his ways, and to keep his commandments, and his statutes, and his judgments, which he commanded our fathers. And let these my words, wherewith I have made supplication before the Lord, be night unto the Lord our God day and night, that he maintain the cause of his servant, and the cause of his people Israel at all times, as the matter shall require: That all the people of the earth may know that the Lord is God, and that there is none else. Let your heart therefore be perfect with the Lord our God, to walk in his statutes, and to keep his commandments, as at this day."

Solomon was blessed by God with great wisdom and realized that following God's commandments, statutes, and laws was paramount in pleasing God. God also gave Solomon a heart that was completely committed to the Lord and obeyed His commands. He realized that to manage all the people of Israel would require a man with an extraordinary sense of justice with the ability to resolve very complicated issues. Solomon's negotiation skills allowed Israel many years of peace as he worked to resolve issues and avoid war with neighboring countries.

Solomon asked for God's blessings to be placed on the land of Israel and its people which resulted in Israel experiencing the blessing of peace, the blessing of wealth, many new government buildings, and God's temple. However, even after great success, Solomon failed to keep God's commandments and turned to worldly pleasures. Solomon's focus turned from worshiping, praising, and thanking God for His many blessings to worshiping possessions, seeking fame, and being consumed by seeking pleasure. Eventually, Solomon's heart was controlled by lust and not the love for his God. Today's culture is still consumed by seeking and accumulating wealth, possessions, fame, status, and pleasure.

Initially, God was pleased with Solomon and his desire to help the people of Israel and build a strong country and ensure a prosperous future

Solomon and Naamah

for Israel. However, as Solomon accumulated more wealth and fame he became a victim to man's basic desire for more fame, more wealth, greed, and self. Man's basic desire is to be recognized by others has a profound effect on how man sees himself and sees others. As Christians we realize all of our wealth belongs to God and our desire is to be more like our Savior each day.

Most people realize that their self worth and self image was partially developed by how other people (including parents) approved or disapproved of their successes or failures. As Christians this baggage is eliminated and replaced with the knowledge that God loves each of us in all of our successes and failures. Our self-worth and self-image is also made complete with the knowledge that God loved each one of us enough to sacrifice His only Son so that we live sin free forever in heaven.

Another issue that contributed to Rehoboam's problems was Solomon's marriages to foreign women. Rehoboam's mother was Naamah (an Ammonitess) who married Solomon and followed other foreign gods.

1 Kings 11:11 reads, "Wherefore the Lord said unto Solomon, Forasmuch as this is done of thee, and thou hast not kept my covenant and my statutes, which I have commanded thee, I will surely rend the kingdom from thee, and will give it to the servant."

Rehoboam would suffer from the sins of his father and be raised by a mother that worshiped foreign gods. To further complicate the issue he would not listen to the elders of the tribes. All of these sins made it impossible for Rehoboam to match the success of his father Solomon.

Exodus 34:12-16 reads, " Take heed to thyself, least thou make a covenant with the inhabitants of the land whither thou guest, least it be for a snare in the midst of thee: But ye shall destroy their altars, break their images, and cut down their groves: For thou shalt worship no other god: for the Lord, whose name is Jealous, is a Jealous God: Lest thou make a covenant with the inhabitants of the land, and they go a whoring after their gods, and do sacrifice unto their gods, and one call thee, and thou eat of his sacrifice: And thou take of their daughters unto thy sons, and their daughters go a whoring after their gods, and make thy sons go a whoring after their gods."

God instructed the Israelites in His statutes not to allow their sons to marry the daughters of foreigners. In addition, God instructed the Israelites to destroy all the images of foreign gods and any related foreign god structures. Solomon and Rehoboam failed to comply with many of God's commandments, statutes, and laws. The result was the separation of Israel into two kingdoms with years of war and unrest.

Rehoboam and Maacah
Approximately (972–913 BC)

REHOBOAM WAS THE SON of King Solomon and the grandson to King David. He ruled over both the northern and southern Kingdoms for a short period of time until the tribes of the northern Kingdom rebelled and broke away. His greed and the heavy tax he levied on the people resulted in a rebellion by ten tribes. Rehoboam did not listen or seek God's wisdom but listened to the council of those that were in his court. The result was disastrous. Rehoboam lost control of the northern kingdom and remained the King for only the southern kingdom of Judah. God's displeasure with Solomon caused the kingdoms to collapse without God's blessings and protection.

1 Kings 11:1-2 reads, "But King Solomon loved many strange women, together with the daughter of Pharaoh, woman of the Moabites, Ammonites, Edomites, Zidonians, and Hittites; Of the nations concerning which the Lord said unto the children of Israel, Ye shall not go in to them, neither shall they come in unto you: for surely they will turn away your heart after their gods: Solomon clave unto these in love."

Solomon's disobedience, Rehoboam's inability and evil rule set into action a series of disasters for the Kingdom of Judah. The King of Egypt brought a huge army against Judah that resulted in Jerusalem and Judah falling under Egyptian rule.

Obviously, God blessed David and Solomon with great wealth and treasures because of their hearts and willingness to follow God's direction. However, Solomon's sin and disobedience quickly resulted in the disappearance of wealth and prosperity for the Jewish people.

Rehabaom and his wife Maacah had the following children; Abijah, Attai, Ziza, and Shelomith. It is believed that Maacah was a very strong-willed evil person and the granddaughter of Absalom.

God's love and His covenant with David allowed Abijah to experience some of God's patience.

APPLICATION

The turning of Solomon away from God during the end of his reign as King of Judah resulted in many dire consequences. Ten tribes revolted due to heavy taxation, the kingdom was split between north (Israel) and south (Judah), and idols were made and worshiped. Solomon's son Rehoboam did not seek God and did not follow His commandments. His rule was reduced to Judah and Jerusalem as the capital. There was also great animosity between the north and south kingdoms that lead to warfare between the two kingdoms for many years.

2 Chronicles 12:14 reads,"And he did evil, because he prepared not his heart to seek the Lord."

Rehoboam ruled Judah for seventeen years and during that time he made many idols for the people to worship the Moabite and Ammonite gods. The practice of marrying foreign women resulted in the introduction of many foreign gods and new worshiping practices.

God's commandments are not requests, suggestions or recommendations, they are God's demands. God is the same today as He was 2000 years ago. God did not change the Ten Commandments when Jesus died on the cross.

John 14:15 reads, "If ye love me, keep my commandments."

For Christians today, keeping God's commandments is a way of showing their love for God and his many blessings. A Christian strives to live a life that is pleasing to God, showing respect for a mighty God and His creation, and showing a never-ending thankfulness for His love and the gift of His Son.

There is only one Bible with the Old Testament accounting for over two thirds of the entire Bible. The birth and death of Jesus Christ was the fulfillment of Old Testament prophecies. Jesus the Christ lived His entire life without sin and fulfilled the requirements for being a perfect lamb for sacrifice to carry all the sin of the world. He followed the Old Testament Commandments and laws. However, Jesus did not comply with all of the

Jewish statutes and customs when He considered them to be unjust. For example, helping an injured animal caught in a snare on the Sabbath would be an act of love and justified.

Both the Old Testament and the New Testament requires Christians to love one another.

Leviticus 19:18 reads, "Thou shalt not avenge, nor bear any grudge against the children of the people, but thou shalt love thy neighbor as thyself: I am the Lord."

John 13:34 reads, "A new commandment I give unto you, That ye love one another as I have loved you, that ye also love one another."

Jesus fulfilled a Mosaic statute when he instructed His disciples as how to love each other. They needed to be willing to lay down their lives for one another just as Jesus laid down His life for all of mankind. Jesus knew that all of these disciples would experience persecution and an early death except for John who was imprisoned for many years.

Rehoboam was part of the royal bloodline and part of the covenant that God made to Abraham and to David.

Genesis 15:18 reads, "In the same day the Lord made a covenant with Abraham, saying, Unto thy seed have I given this land, from the river of Egypt unto the great river, the river Euphrates:"

Acts 13:22-23 reads ,"And when he had removed him, he raised up unto them David to be their king; to whom also he gave testimony, and said, I HAVE FOUND DAIVD the son of Jesse, A MAN AFTER MINE OWN HEART, which shall fulfill all my will. Of this man's seed hath God according to his promise raised unto Israel a Savior, Jesus:"

Revelation 22:16 reads, "I Jesus have sent mine angel to testify unto you these things in the churches. I am the root and the offspring of David, and the bright and morning star."

God made a promise to David that he would see his descendant, Jesus the Christ sitting upon His throne. David understood this promise and wrote about it in one of his Psalms.

Psalm 89:34-36 reads, "My covenant will I not break, nor alter the thing that is gone out of my lips. Once have I sworn by my holiness that I will not lie unto David. His seed shall endure forever, and his throne as the sun before me."

God promised that His covenant with David would last forever along with His love and faithfulness. If man disobeys God's commandments he would be disciplined. This promise was kept with the birth, death, and resurrection of our Lord, Jesus the Christ.

Abijah and wife unknown
Approximately (913–911 BC)

ABIJAH'S THREE YEAR REIGN began with the death of his father Rehoboam in 913 BC. Abijah's short reign was the result of his death due to unknown reasons.

1 Kings 15:1-4 reads, "Now in the eighteenth year of king Jeroboam the son of Nebat reigned Abijam over Judah. Three years reigned he in Jerusalem. And his mother's name was Maachah, the daughter of Abishalom. And he walked in all the sins of his father, which he had done before him: and his heart was not perfect with the Lord his God, as the heart of David his father. Nevertheless for David's sake did the Lord his God give him a lamp in Jerusalem, to set up his son after him, and to establish Jerusalem:"

King Abijah like his father Rehoboam did not have a close relationship with God. Neither had the close relationship David had with God. However, because of God's close relationship with David God did provide a lamp to Abijah that would provide some light and allow Abijah some wisdom. There are some that believe that Abijah's wife was Arsah.

APPLICATION

There were a number of people named Abijah in the Bible that are both male and female. The Abijah in this case was in David's bloodline, son of Rehoboam and was the king of Judah. During this time there was a great many disagreements between the north (Israel) and south (Judah) kingdoms. Both the king of Judah (Abijah) and the king of the Israel massed great numbers in their armies (400,000) in Judah and (800,000) in Israel.

2 Chronicles 13: 15-16 reads, "Then the men of Judah gave a shout: and as the men of Judah shouted, it came to pass, that God smote Jeroboam

and all Israel before Abijah and Judah. And the children of Israel fled before Judah: and God delivered them into their hand."

2 Chronicles 13:20 reads, "Neither did Jeroboam recover strength again in the days of Abijah: and the Lord struck him, and he died."

King Jeroboam and the northern kingdom were for many years deeply involved in idol worship and other types of perversions. This resulted in God's anger and the loss of over 500,000 men in King Jeroboam's army. However, Abijah made many of the same mistakes as his father Rehoboam and was never able to consolidate the north and south kingdoms.

Jeroboam and the north kingdom worshiped a number of idols rather than worship the one true God. Today, many do worship the one true God, but millions still refuse to believe that God exists. These people live out their lives searching for meaning and purpose for their lives in many different ways. Materialism is the most popular with millions looking for validation with larger homes, expensive cars, and closets and storage space with things. Satan and man's fallen nature makes these people victims to a cruel trap. This insatiable desire for more has no end and only leads to greed, pride, and envy. The worship of idols has been replaced by the worship of self.

Exodus 20:17 reads, "Thou shalt not covet thy neighbor's house, thou shalt not covet thy neighbor's wife, not his manservant, nor his maidservant, nor his ox, nor his ass, nor anything that is thy neighbor's."

We live in a worldwide consumer economy where companies and organizations come and go with the demand for their products and services. Billions of dollars are spent by these companies and organizations each year in marketing their products and services. The marketing methods and strategies used today are extremely sophisticated and target man's many weaknesses. Unfortunately, the poor and unsophisticated are the first to fall pray to these dishonest and misleading marketing programs.

As companies face stiffer competition in a world market and as they fight to stay alive they are willing to take advantage of every opportunity regardless of who falls prey. One common marketing ploy is to set in motion the idea that people are somehow in competition with their neighbors and that they should covet their neighbor's possessions. This strike at man's basic weaknesses as it's relates to pride, envy, and self.

1 Timothy 6:6-12 reads,"But godliness with contentment is great gain. For we brought nothing into this world, and it is certain we can carry nothing out. And having food and raiment let us be therewith content. But they

that will be rich fall into temptation and a snare, and into many foolish and hurtful lusts, which drown men in destruction and perdition. For the love of money is the root of all evil: which while some coveted after, they have erred from the faith, and pierced themselves through with many sorrows. But thou, O man of God, flee these things; and follow after righteousness, godliness, faith, love, patience, meekness. Fight the good fight of faith, lay hold on eternal life, whereunto thou art also called, and hast professed a good profession before many witnesses. I give thee charge to the sight of God, who quickeneth all things, and before Christ Jesus, who before Pontius Pilate witnessed a good confession;"

Very seldom do you hear people thank God for His many blessings. Most people are not content with their lives and are on a continual treadmill of complaints and dissatisfaction with all they encounter on a daily basis (i.e., spouse, job, house, children).

The fall of mankind resulted in the separation between God and man and the resulting void. From that point forward man has been trying to fill that void with money, possessions, travel, status, relationships, etc. This void is filled with contentment and happiness when God is allowed to take charge of our lives. God and His Holy Spirit are waiting for each person to pray the prayer of admitting they are a sinner and are in need of forgiveness.

The solution to many of life's problems is simply to follow God's commandments. Loving God with all your heart and loving your neighbor as yourself will prevent your heart from loving yourself.

Matthew 22:37-40 reads, "Jesus said unto him, Thou Shalt Love The Lord Thy God With All Thy Heart, And With All Thy Soul, And With All Thy Mind. This is the first and great commandment. And the second is like unto it, Thou Shalt Love Thy Neighbor As Thyself. On these two commandments hang all the law and the prophets."

Asa and Azubah
Approximately (911–870 BC)

KING ASA WAS GENERALLY considered a righteous king due to the fact he ensured that many of the idols and places of idol worship were destroyed.

1 Kings 15:8-11 reads, "And Abijah slept with his fathers; and they buried him in the city of David: And Asa his son reigned in his stead. And in the twentieth year of Jeroboam king of Israel reigned Asa over Judah. And forty and one years reigned he in Jerusalem, And his mother's name was Maachah, the daughter of Abishalom. And Asa did that which was right in the eyes of the Lord, as did David his father."

King Asa and his spouse Azubah had a son Jehoshaphat who became Asa's successor in about 870 BC.

2 Chronicles 15: 10-12 reads, "So they gathered themselves together at Jerusalem in the third month, in the fifteenth year of the reign of Asa. And they offered unto the Lord the same time, of the spoil which they had brought, seven hundred oxen and seven thousand sheep. And they entered into a covenant to seek the Lord God of their fathers with all their heart and with all their soul;"

King Asa assembled worshipers of the one true God and made a promise to follow and obey the laws of the Jewish people. He made a great sacrifice of the animals that had been taken as the spoil of wars. God rewarded Asa and the Jewish people with peace for a period of time.

APPLICATION

Asa was the third king of the southern kingdom of Judah and reversed many of the evil practices of his father, Abijah and grandfather, Rehoboam. His rule lasted for forty one years.

2 Chronicles 14:2 reads, "And Asa did that which was good and right in the eyes of the Lord his God."

2 Chronicles 15:1 reads, "And the spirit of God came upon Azariah the son of Oded: An he went out to meet Asa, and said unto him, Hear ye me, Asa, and all Judah and Benjamin; The Lord is with you, while ye be with him; and if ye seek him, he will be found of you; but if ye forsake him, he will forsake you."

God used the prophet Azariah to encourage Asa to move forward with getting rid of the idols and encouraging the people to worship the one true God. However, Asa made mistakes toward the end of his rule when he entered into treaties with ungodly kings. The result was war and oppression for many of the people.

Jehoshaphat the son of Asa followed his father and became a godly king and ruled for 25 years. However, both Asa and his son Jehoshaphat made mistakes toward the end of their reigns as their dedication to God waivered. It is important that we remain steadfast in our faith and are aware how easy it is to be distracted by the world and it's many temptations.

The lesson to be learned from these kings is the importance of bringing all issues to God in prayer and to maintain an unwavering relationship with God throughout your entire life. The Holy Spirit works with all men in directing their paths and fulfilling their individual mission throughout their lives. The greatest danger that lies in wait for man is self and the weakness not to trust God, but to solve life's issues with personal knowledge and past experience. As King Asa, some people actually depend on a consensus of opinions from other people that may or may not be believers.

The first priority in this life is to praise God for His love, grace, and many blessings. We need to ask for God's blessings and protection each day for ourselves and our entire family. We live in a dangerous world where we can encounter harm from any number of different sources. We bring all of our decisions before God in prayer and take no action without first asking for God's blessings. God may bring other people into our lives that will assist in pointing us in the right direction. God can also direct our lives by making new opportunities available, limiting options, and changing priorities.

Today, we live under the guidance of the Holy Spirit that was given to us after the death and resurrection of Jesus Christ. It is prayer and the study of the scriptures that allows our hearts and mind to be lead by the Holy Spirit. The Holy Spirit will intercede for those who search His word and pray for God's blessings. As believers we are locked into a lifelong relationship with the Holy Spirit that if allowed will grow with an increased depth of spiritual knowledge and blessings in terms of maturity in ourselves and others.

Our lives are an endless series of decisions that can determine success or failure. The smallest carefree decision can release a catastrophic series of events that change our lives forever. God will hold us responsible for our decisions and we will need to accept the consequences for each word, action, and thought. We desperately need the Holy Spirit to guide us through each decision, each word and each thought.

Psalm 34:9-10 reads, "O fear the Lord, ye his saints: for there is no want to them that fear him. The young lions do lack, and suffer hunger: but they that seek the Lord shall not want any good thing."

As Christians we are subject to the pressures from an immoral society that demands we conform to its values and worship of it's idols of sexual perversion, material consumption, and the worship of self.

Jehoshaphat and wife unknown
Approximately (907–848 BC)

JEHOSPHAPHAT THE SON OF Asa ruled over Judah for 25 years and was the fourth King of Judah. King Jehoshaphat's son Jehoram was the oldest of seven sons and would succeed him as King. It is generally agreed that Judah did experience a great many blessings, prosperity, and peace because of Jehoshaphat's desire to teach the law and free the land of Idol worship. At this time Israel the neighbor to the north was plagued with idol worship and kings that were not focused on God's will.

It was Jehosphaphat's rule and focus to eliminate pagan worship that allowed God's blessings to be realized in terms of military security, a time of peace, and education of the law. These new measures included seeking God's will and approval before making any decisions or takng any actions. Jehoshaphat's rule also included establishing a system of judges and courts in each of the major cities that allowed people access to resolving their disputes.

2 Chronicles 19:4-7 reads, "And Johoshaphat dwelt at Jerusalem: and he went out again through the people from Beer-sheba to mount Ephraim, and brought them back unto the Lord God of their fathers. And he set judges in the land throughout all the fenced cities of Judah, city by city, And said to the judges, Take heed what ye do: for ye judge not for man, but for the Lord, who is with you in the Judgment. Wherefore now let the fear of the Lord be upon you: take heed and do it: for there is no iniquity with the Lord our God, nor respect of person, nor taking of gifts."

God richly blessed Johoshaphat and his rule because he put God first before all decisions, he was depended on God for direction, and he feared God knowing God is the final judge.

Jehoshaphat and wife unknown

2 Chronicles 20: 18-20 reads, "And Johoshaphat bowed his head with his face to the ground: and all Judah and the inhabitants of Jerusalem fell before the Lord, worshipping the Lord. And Levites, of the children of the Kohathites, and of the children of the Korhites, stood up to praise the Lord God of Israel with a lord voice on high. And they rose early in the morning, and went forth into the wilderness of Tekoa: and as they went forth, Jehoshaphat stood and said, Hear me, O Judah, and ye inhabitants of Jerusalem; Believe in the Lord your God, so shall ye be established; believe his prophets, so shall ye prosper."

A great army of Ammon and Moab stood up against Judah and was going to attack when God intervened and caused the armies to fight among themselves that eventually ended in destroying each other. Johoshapat and the people of Judah spent three days collecting the riches left by the invading armies. God was pleased with Johoshapat and the people of Judah and blessed them greatly as they turned to worshiping God and seeking His path for their daily lives.

During this same time period the Northern Kingdom of Israel was ruled by many kings involved in the worship of pagan gods. Many of these kings of the Northern Kingdom of Israel required the worship of pagan gods because of the financial benefits realized from the people's sacrifices. One of the wickedest kings during this time period was King Ahab and his wife Jezebel. During their reign temples were built for the purpose of unspeakable acts of human depravity and human sacrifices.

Elijah (Approx. 900 BC) was a prophet that had many frailties who was completely dependent on God for his daily existence. God blessed Elijah in many ways as he carried out God's mission and was obedient to God's commands and direction. God protected Elijah from King Ahad and his wife Jezebel who sent out soldiers to kill him after he confronted the King about his intention to force people to worship pagan gods and Elijah's prophecy of a three year drought. Elijah's life was under God's protection and blessings as God lead Elijah to safety and revealed His grace through a poor widow and her young son.

At this point in time the population surrounding the Mediterranean area was deeply involved in worshiping pagan gods, mythology, and other types of superstitions. There was a keen interest on the part of governments, kings, and temple priests to encourage and support these practices for as long as possible. A great deal of social infrastructure was financially dependent on the buying and selling of approved sacrifices and other related business. Governments and temple priests were able to accumulate great wealth to build massive temples and other pagan worship facilities. Governments, kings and temple priests took advantage of the general population's superstitions by promoting the idea that the greater the sacrifice the greater the blessings. In some cases, the worship of pagan gods was mandatory and people were put to death for not worshiping pagan gods or pledging funds to the pagan temple.

Breaking this strangle hold on the people of Israel would require God to use Elijah to perform a great miracle that would discredit the pagan gods, the pagan priests and King Ahab.

APPLICATION

Jehoshaphat recognized the danger of being located near to Israel and all the evil that was being encouraged and promoted by the worship of pagan gods. He built strong fortifications along the border with Israel and took on the task of purging Judah of all pagan gods and all their worshiping practices. Jehoshaphat sent out priests and Levites to instruct the people as to how to follow the law. This initial effort to cleanse Judah of all the pagan worship and all the related superstitions resulted in receiving God's blessings. These blessings came in the form of peace, prosperity, and a bountiful harvest. However, like many other kings of Judah mistakes were made by Jehoshaphat when he relied on himself and others for council rather than go to God for direction. In some situations, Jehoshaphat actually entered into alliances with Ahab, king of the northern kingdom. Ahab was one of evilest kings of the northern kingdom and did take advantage of Jehoshaphat and his misplaced trust.

Jehoshaphat carried the royal bloodline forward of the Messiah with instructing the people how to worship the one true God and how to follow and keep His commandments.

Today, evil runs rampant as it destroys and rips apart families and society. Evil uses man's weakness for greed, envy, and self to divide people into groups that fight each other over many different issues. God became man to unite man to God and to form one unit. Evil works to destroy marriages, communities, and all other units that promote love, cooperation, respect, and understanding.

1 John 5:19 reads, "And we know that we are of God, and the whole world lieth in wickedness."

2 Corinthians 4:4 reads, "In whom the god of this world hath blinded the minds of them which believe not, lest the light of the glorious gospel of the Christ, who is the image of God, should shine unto them."

Throughout history man has needed to choose between good and evil and God and Satan. God has allowed Satan to be part of the world and is the reason for sin, disease and death. The freedom to choose between good and evil allows love to be created in a world that would otherwise be buried in sin.

As Christians we live in a world that is not our home. We must continually resist Satan and make every effort to grow closer to God our Savior. We should work through each day in recognizing our sins and confessing them in prayer to God and ask for forgiveness.

All men are flawed and are in need of a Savior. Jesus Christ came to this world because he understood man's flawed character and loved all of mankind regardless of his many flaws. God gave His only Son as the complete and final sacrifice for all of man's sin. It is a free gift that is available to all of mankind simply through faith.

Ephesians 6:10-20 reads, "Finally, my brethren, be strong in the Lord, and in the power of his might. Put on the whole armor of God, that ye may be able to stand against the wiles of the devil. For we wrestle not against flesh and blood, but against principalities, against powers, against the rulers of the darkness of this world, against spiritual wickedness in high places. Wherefore take unto you the whole armor of God, that ye may be able to withstand in the evil day, and having done all, to stand. Stand therefore, having your loins girt about with truth and having on the breastplate of righteousness. And on your feet shod with the preparation of the gospel of peace; Above all, taking the shield of faith, wherewith ye shall be able to quench all the fiery darts of the wicked. And take the helmet of salvation, and the sword of the Spirit, which is the word of God. Praying always with all prayer and supplication in the Spirit, and watching thereunto with all perseverance and supplication for all saints; And for me, that utterance may be given unto me, that I may open my mouth boldly, to make known the mystery of the gospel. For which I am an ambassador in bonds: that therein I may speak boldly, as I ought to speak."

Jehoshaphat carried the royal bloodline forward of the Messiah and was blessed by God. However, he was still subject to the fiery darts of Satan and the rulers of the darkness. As Christians we are able withstand the attacks of Satan and all spiritual wickedness because of the truth that lives within us. We are covered by the saving grace of God, the salvation that was made possible with the death and resurrection of God's only Son, Jesus Christ, and the Holy Spirit that carries our prayers forward. We spend our waking hours thanking and praising God for His many blessings and showing His love to others.

Like Jehoshaphat, many Christians underestimate the power of Satan and how he is able to influence all of mankind. His primary objective is to destroy all of God's creation (all of mankind) and will use any means to achieve his goals. Each day we see Satan's influence as he uses lying and slander to divide and destroy the world and all of mankind.

Romans 16:17 reads, "Now I beseech you, brethren, mark them which cause divisions and offenses contrary to the doctrine which ye have learned; and avoid them."

1 Corinthians 6:18-19 reads, "Flee fornication. Every sin that a men doeth is without the body; but he that committed fornication sinneth against his own body." What? know ye not that your body is the temple of the Holy Ghost which is in you, which ye have of God, and ye are not your own?"

Christians need to flee sin and not entertain those that are involved in a life that is devoted to promoting a sinful life style. Today, Christians grossly underestimate the power and the influence of Satan and will make allowances and conform to social pressures as to avoid being placed in an unpopular position. A faith that is compromised will damage not only your own soul and your relationship with the Holy Spirit, but will also work as a cancer that will spread through all of your family and friends.

Jehoram and Athaliah
Approximately (882– 842 BC)

IT IS BELIEVED THAT King Jehoram began his short reign of 8 years at the age of 32. There was a great deal of turmoil in Judah during his reign and he responded by forming an alliance with the northern kingdom of Israel. This alliance was created when he married Athaliah the daughter of King Ahab of the northern kingdom of Israel. However, many revolted against his rule and found their independence from King Jehoram of Judah.

2 Chronicles 21: 8-10 reads, "In his days the Edomites revolted from under the domination of Judah, and made themselves a king. Then Jehoram went forth with his princes, and all his chariots with him: and he rose up by night, and smote the Edomites which compassed him in, and the captains of the chariots. So the Edomites revolted from under the hand of Judah unto this day. The same time also did Libnah revolt from under his hand; because he had forsaken the Lord God of His fathers."

Again we see a king that did not rely on God for direction but fell to the worship of pagan gods and other evil that had infected the north kingdom of Israel. Jerhoram's sin included killing his brothers and others that threatened his reign. The result of his sin was a short life, a painful death, and Jerusalem being plundered and the temple ransacked. However, God still maintained his covenant with King David and Judah and allowed the Messiah bloodline to continue.

This is one more example of a king that refused to obey God's law and commandments and then had to suffer the consequences. God does react to sin and will discipline those that fall short and sin. God is a God of love and will discipline out of love those that sin.

Sin will lead to disease and death. Sin is a trap that will entice you with a short period of pleasure and joy and will follow with long term periods of pain, grief, and suffering.

Romans 6:23 reads, "For the wages of sin is death, but the gift of God is eternal life through Jesus Christ our Lord."

Sin will lead to the death of both the soul and body. The only escape from sin and its consequences is to believe in the gift of God's only Son, Jesus Christ that was freely given for all of mankind that was born in sin. It was Adam's disobedience that resulted in changing the relationship between mankind and God. The introduction of sin caused life to change in many ways for both men and women. The disobedience to God's word and commandments would now result in death, life would be limited to a number of years, and God would send His only Son as a free gift and a way to escape the burden of man's sin.

Romans 5:12-17 reads, "Wherefore, as by one man sin entered into the world, and death by sin; and so death passed upon all men, for that all have sinned: For until the law sin was in the world: but sin is not imputed when there is no law. Nevertheless death reigned from Adam to Moses, even over them that had not sinned after the similitude of Adam's transgressions, who is the figure of him that was to come. But not as the offence, so also is the free gift. For if through the offense of one many be dead, much more the grace of God, and the gift by grace, which is by one man, Jesus Christ, hath abounded unto many. And not as it was by one that sinned, so is the gift: for the judgment was by one to condemnation, but the free gift is of many offenses unto justification. For if by one man's offense death reigned by one; much more they which receive abundance of grace and of the gift of righteousness shall reign in life by one, Jesus Christ."

The sin of Adam resulted in the sinful nature of all mankind and death. From that time forward all men would be burdened with a sinful nature and subject to death. However, Jesus Christ was able to break the shakes of death that allowed all of mankind a path to salvation from the sting of death and to an eternal life of grace.

APPLICATION

King Jehoram was one more king that failed and worshiped idols. Jehoram's alliance with the northern kingdom and his marriage to King Ahab's daughter accomplish little and did not protect him from disease and a painful death.

2 Corinthians 6:14 reads, "Be ye not unequally yoked together with unbelievers: for what fellowship hath righteousness with unrighteousness? And what communion hath light with darkness?"

God has commanded us that we do not enter into a partnership with a person who has rejected God. To proceed in this type of relationship is a sin and we will suffer the consequences. We all have seen many of these alliances between believers and non-believers and have witnessed the resulting pain and complications that in some cases last for generations.

We are witnesses to these painful relationships and are often placed in awkward situations where opinions are freely given. Jesus the Christ instructed us not to make judgments and not think of ourselves as superior to these individuals.

Mathew 7:1-2 reads, "Judge not that ye be not judged. For with what judgment ye judge, ye shall be judged: and with what measure ye mete, it shall be measured to you again."

In other words, do not judge others or you will be judged in the same way. Again we see how God holds us directly responsible for our actions and the direct relationship between sin and discipline. However, Jesus takes the issue of judgment to another step and that step addresses being a hypocrite. Man's flawed character and Satan's powerful influence has placed natural man in a thick fog where truth is lost and men attack each other for little or no reason.

God also provides other commands that address the difference between judgment and discernment.

Matthew 7:6 reads, "Give not that which is holy unto the dogs, neither cast ye your pearls before swine, lest they trample them under their feet, and turn again and rent you."

We need to use discernment in witnessing to those that repeatedly reject God's message and continue to live a life that ridicules God's word and the gospel. Jesus found these individuals repulsive and compared them to swine wallowing in mud. Jesus came to the world to save the sinner and would eat with both sinners and tax collectors. He shared the gospel with all and gave all the opportunity to believe in Him as their Savior and Lord. However, He would move on if not welcomed by those that refused to believe.

Matthew 10:14 reads, "And whosoever shall not receive you, nor hear your words, when ye depart out of that house or city, shake off the dust of your feet."

There are people who spend years stuck in the mud trying to force others to believe in the gospel and at the same time ignoring those waiting to hear the saving words of grace and wasting precious time. We are responsible for sharing the message for the gospel, but it is only the Holy Spirit that convicts the soul of man.

Christians today that have been sealed by the Holy Spirit and love their Savior and Lord, spend each day trying to live a life that is pleasing to God.

Ephesians 4:30 reads, "And grieve not the holy Spirit of God, whereby ye are sealed unto the day of redemption."

The Holy Spirit directs our lives through scripture study and will direct us as a guide and counselor. However, it is possible to grieve the Holy Spirit with sin. To maintain and build a strong relationship with God's Spirit will obviously require us to run from sin and spend time in study. As we clear our minds of sin and the idols of the world we begin to open the door and allow the Holy Spirit to take a more activity role in our daily lives.

Today we find ourselves in a world that is lost in a fog that prevents men from seeing the value in living a spiritual life and respecting God's word and His plan for their lives.

King Jehoram was also lost and fell prey to the social pressures of worshiping idols and not accepting God and His commandments. The idols of today are also only temporary and will be forgotten as future generations of non-believers select different idols and waste their lives chasing perceived pleasures related to things.

The Gospel of Matthew
Genealogy–Matt: 1:1–17

IT IS BELIEVED AT this point in the genealogy the Apostle Mathew does not include certain kings. It is believed that Ahaziah, Joash, and Amaziah were not mentioned for unknown reasons. Mathew a tax collector became an Apostle early in Jesus' ministry in Capernaum. He was viewed as an agent of the Roman government and was despised by the Jewish population. Regardless of Matthew's standing in the community, Matthew was selected by Jesus to be one of His disciples and a witness to the Ascension.

Acts 1: 9-14 reads, "And when he had spoken these things, while they beheld he was taken up; and a cloud received him out of their sight. And while they looked steadfastly toward heaven as he went up, two men stood by them in white apparel; Which also said, Ye men of Galilee, why stand ye gazing up into heaven? This same Jesus, which is taken up from you into heaven, shall so come in like manner as ye have seen him go into heaven. Then returned they unto Jerusalem from the mount called Olivet, which is from Jerusalem a sabbath day's journey. And when they were come in, they went up into an upper room, where abode both Peter, and James, and John, and Andrew, Philip, and Thomas, Bartholomew, and Matthew, James the son of Alpheus, and Simon Zelotes, and Judas the brother of James. These all continued with one accord in prayer and supplication, with the women, and Mary the mother of Jesus, and with his brethren."

Matthew was a witness to Jesus' resurrection and ascension. He understood that Jesus would return as prophesied and that he would be from the house of David.

Uzziah and Jerusha
Approximately (808–740BC)

KING UZZIAH BEGAN HIS reign at the age of 16 and served as king for 52 years. It is believed that King Uzziah was a faithful servant to the one true God and was under the influence of the prophet Zechariah.

2 Kings 15:3 reads, "And he did that which was right in the sight of the Lord, according to all that his father Amaziah had done."

His reign was blessed by God and the people and Judah prospered because King Uzziah obeyed God's word and commands. The army was rebuilt and the city of Jerusalem was fortified to repeal enemy invasions. King Uzziah was a very successful and prosperous king until his pride became an issue.

2 Chronicles 26: 18-19 reads, "And they withstood Uzziah the King, and said unto him, It appertaineth not unto thee, Uzziah, to burn incense unto the Lord, but to the priests the sons of Aaron, that are consecrated to burn incense: go out of the sanctuary; for thou hast trespassed; neither shall it be for thine honor from the Lord God. Then Uzziah was wroth, and had a censer in his hand to burn incense: and while he was wroth with the priests, the leprosy even rose up in his forehead before the priests in the house of the Lord, from beside the incense alter."

King Uzziah was filled with pride because of his many successes and accomplishments. He did not realize that these accomplishments were due to God's many blessings. In other words, he allowed pride and self to take credit for the prosperity of Judah rather than to thank God for his many blessings. The result of this sin came in the form of disease and death. King Uzziah was struck down with leprosy and suffered under the pain of the disease for many years. His reign as King was turned over to his son Jotham and the two reigned for eleven years together until his death.

We see in this example that Uzziah's sin had a direct impact on his life and others around him. We also see that God will respond quickly and harshly to self, ego, and the pride of life. It is one sin that is mentioned many times throughout God's word. However, there are also examples of God disciplining his people in a loving way to stretch them and strengthen their witness.

Hebrews 12:6 reads, "For Whom the Lord Loveth He Chasteneth, and Scourgeth Every Son Whom He Receiveth."

All of God's children are subject to His loving discipline. We are all sinners and we will all experience God' discipline in some way and in His time.

APPLICATION

A Christian's life is a life of faith and is subject to God's loving discipline as a father disciplines his children.

Hebrews 12: 5-11 reads, "And ye have forgotten the exhortation which speaketh unto you as unto children, My son, despise not thou the chastening of the Lord, nor faint when thou art rebuked of him: For whom the Lord loveth He chasteneth, and scourgeth every son whom he receiveth. If ye endure chastening, God dealeth with you as with sons; for what son is he whom the father chasteneth not? But if ye be without chastisement, whereof all are partakers, then are ye bastards, and not sons. Furthermore we have had fathers of our flesh which corrected us, and we gave them reverence: shall we not much rather be in subjection unto the Father of spirits, and live? For they verily for a few days chastened us after their own pleasure; but he for our profit, that we might be partakers of his holiness. Now no chastening for the present seemeth to be joyous, but grievous: nevertheless afterwards it yieldeth the peaceable fruit of righteousness unto them which are exercised thereby."

As Christians and sons of God we should take God's discipline with an attitude of thanksgiving realizing He loves us and wants to build within us righteousness. Going through God's discipline is painful and can lead to despair and sorrow. However, those who are able to learn from discipline receive great rewards and the sons of God receive the peace of righteousness that is beyond our understanding.

2 Timothy 4:7 reads, "I have fought a good fight, I have finished my course, I have kept the faith:"

2 Timothy 3:12 reads, "Yea, and all that will live godly in Christ Jesus shall suffer persecution."

Believers in Christ live a courageous and uncompromising life and will at times be subject to the sin and evil that the world has to offer. God is in control of the world and will allow his children to suffer when it is to the benefit of the believer. As Christians we all go through our individual transformation to righteousness that is specifically designed for our individual character.

We need to be in continual prayer with our Lord and Savior to allow the Holy Spirit to speak for us and gain a better understanding of God's leading and how He is preparing us to meet our Creator.

The sin of Adam had a monumental impact on man's life on this earth.

Genesis 3:17-19 reads, "And unto Adam he said, Because thou hast hearkened unto the voice of thy wife, and hast eaten of the tree, of which I commanded thee, saying, thou shalt not eat of it: cursed is the ground for thy sake; in sorrow shalt thou eat of it all the days of thy life; Thorns also and thistles shall it bring forth to thee; and thou shalt eat the herb of the field: In the sweat of thy face shalt thou eat bread, till thou return unto the ground: for out of it wast thou taken: for dust thou art, and unto dust shalt thou return."

We live in a fallen world that exposes us to many different challenges, many of which we have little or no control over. We have seen natural disasters that have taken the lives of many and impacted millions of others without warning. God allowed plagues to take place in Egypt that destroyed the land and shorten the life of many.

The truth is that we wake up each morning not knowing what is going to happen in this world we live in. We are all going to die and some are going to live longer than others due to God's plan for each individual's life. Our focus should be on praising God for the gift of His Son that allows us to live forever with Him in heaven.

King Uzziah had a long reign and God allowed him to carry the royal bloodline forward. However, he had many frailties one of which was the sin of pride. Pride is a sin that has been an issue for man since the beginning and is directly related to Satan. We cannot let our guard down and be careful not to allow pride or the worship of idols into our lives.

Jotham and Ahio
Approximately (773–735 BC)

KING JOTHAM FOLLOWED THE teaching and instructions that were given by the prophets Isaiah, Hosea, Amos, and Micah. He was about 25 years old when began his reign for 16 years. He inherited a very prosperous kingdom that was built by his father, King Uzziah and God's blessings. King Jotham feared God and was obedient to God's commands and was careful to listen to the prophets and follow their instructions.

2 Kings 15:32-34 reads, "In the second year of Pekah the son of Remaliah king of Israel began Jotham the son of Uzziah king of Judah to reign. Five and twenty years old was he when he began to reign, and he reigned sixteen years in Jerusalem. And his mother's name was Jerusha, the daughter of Zadok. And he did that which was right in the sight of the Lord: he did according to all that his father Uzziah had done."

God was pleased with King Jotham, but not with the people at this time. The people of Judah were still making sacrifices at the temple and some were still worship pagan gods.

APPLICATION

King Jotham was considered a godly king. Unfortunately, the people of Judah were still involved in worshiping idols.

Leviticus 26:1 reads, "Ye shall make you no idols nor graven image, neither rear you up a standing image, neither shall ye set up any image of stone in your land, to bow down unto it: for I am the Lord your God."

A total surrender to God requires your love and obedience and is void of any worship of any form of idol.

Ezekiel 14:13 reads, " Son of man, when the land sinneth against me by trespassing grievously, then will I stretch out mine hand upon it, and will break the staff of the bread thereof, and will send famine upon it, and will cut off man and beast from it:"

The ultimate betrayal of God is idol worship in its many forms. God finds idol worship extremely repugnant and will cause His wrath to be inflicted upon countries, man, and beast.

Today very few people are worshiping idols in the older sense. Self and pride of life has taken over as the idols for the people in today's world. Many deny the existence of God and in some respects have become completely independent of any religion and worship only self, wealth, pleasure, and possessions. They are addicted to pleasing self and will lie, steal, and kill to satisfy their greed and need for pleasure. The addiction for self pleasure has grown so great that any respect for another person will be ignored if considered an obstacle. The killing of another person is common today as the god of materialism and Satan has taken control over man and his insatiable desire for more possessions. Our prisons are over-crowded with people who have robbed the elderly, killed a child, or committed some kind of mind-numbing crime.

Satan has placed many people in the position where they are lost in a fog where materialism is their god. They exist for the sole purpose of building larger homes and to fill those homes with more and more possessions. This desire for more is in fact covetousness. People today covet larger homes, more possessions, and greater wealth. Satan takes advance of man's weaknesses and traps him in an endless journey for more that only ends in death.

Mathew 22:37 reads, "Jesus said unto him, Thou shalt love the Lord thy God with all thy heart, and with all thy soul, and with all thy mind."

A Christian's life is completely committed to loving God with his entire being. This type of love leaves no room for idols and today's materialism.

Ahaz and Abijah
Approximately (735–715 BC)

KING AHAZ WAS A detestable king that was involved in many evil pagan practices. He began his reign in Judah at the age of 20 years old and reigned for sixteen years. He followed many of the pagan practices of the northern kingdom of Israel and its kings. It is believed that he actually sacrificed one of his sons. Because of King Ahaz's wickedness he died at the age of 36 and was not buried in the sepulcher of the kings.

The prophet Isaiah did provide assistance to King Ahaz by recommending that he listen to God's direction and not that of the rulers of the northern kingdom of Israel and other foreign kingdoms. He refused to listen to Isaiah and follow God's direction.

2 Chronicles 28:27 reads, "And Ahaz slept with his fathers, and they buried him in the city, even in Jerusalem: but they brought him not into the sepulchers of the kings of Israel: and Hezekiah his son reigned in his stead."

We are required to live a life that is righteous and to follow God's commandments and law.

Deuteronomy 6:25 reads, "And it shall be our righteousness, if we observe to do all these commandments before the Lord our God, as he hath commanded us."

Our very survival depends on obeying God's commandments and fearing the Lord God Almighty. We are His creation and the life we live we live in complete obedience with thanksgiving, and praise for His never ending grace.

APPLICATION

The bloodline of the Messiah does include many sinners that in many cases did experience God's discipline and wrath. Those men like King Ahaz do exist for a short period of time and are then cast into a pit to spend eternity with others who refused to obey God's commandments.

At first glance it is difficult to understand how God could use evil for good. However, after further review there appears to be many situations where God has used sinners for His purpose. Joseph is a good example of where evil was used to bring about a blessing.

Genesis 50:20 reads, "But as for you, ye thought evil against me; but God meant it unto good, to bring to pass, as it is this day, to save much people alive."

God's plan for Joseph unfolded as He allowed Joseph to be sold into slavery and delivered to Egypt. God's sovereignty over all of mankind in many ways is beyond our comprehension. In this situation God took the festering sin of jealousy generated by Satan and his brothers and used it as a means to place Joseph in Egypt. In Egypt God would use Joseph to assist his brothers and the Israelites as they found new homes and as the tribes grew in numbers.

We live in a world that is consumed by evil and acts of wickedness are performed throughout each day. God has allowed this evil to exist and will use it for His purpose and in His time. God has also given man free will and the ability to love God by choosing to obey God's commands and refuse to follow Satan and a life of sin.

Colossians 2:15 reads, "And having spoiled principalities and powers, he made a show of them openly, triumphing over them in it."

The crucifixion of Jesus and His resurrection defeated Satan and his fallen angels. It was Jesus a man who lived a sin free life and his death and resurrection that defeated sin, death, Satan and his powers.

Romans 8:28. Reads, "And we know that all things work together for good to them that love God, to them who are the called according to his purpose."

We worship and obey the one true God that is all knowing, eternal in existence, and controls all things for His purpose under His grace. He is the one and only true God that is the Creator of the universe and is able to have a personal relationship with those who believe in His name. He is able to forgive the sin for those who come to Him and ask for forgiveness and obey His commandments.

Hezekiah and Hephzibah
Approximately (739– 686 BC)

Hezekiah was king during a time period when he witnessed the destruction of the northern kingdom of Israel in about 722 BC by the Assyrians. Both Isaiah and Micah were prophets during this time period. Hezekiah was also responsible for ensuring that Judah would only worship the one true God and purged the temple of all other gods. He was a great and God fearing king of Judah.

However, King Hezekiah made the fatal error of not going to God first before making the decision to begin negotiations with the King of Assyria that lead to complete destruction.

2 Kings 18:15-16 reads, "And Hezekiah gave him all the silver that was found in the house of the Lord, and in the treasures of the king's house. At that time did Hezekiah cut off the gold from the doors of the temple of the Lord, and from the pillars which Hezekiah king of Judah had overlaid, and gave it to the king of Assyria."

The king of Assyria was not satisfied with the silver and gold sent by Hezekiah and sent his army to demand that Hezekiah surrender. The king of Assyria also blasphemed the Lord and did experience God's wrath when He destroyed his army

Isaiah 37: 35-37 reads, "For I will defend this city to save it for mine own sake, and for my servant David's sake. Then the angle of the Lord went forth, and smote in the camp of the Assyrians a hundred and fourscore and five thousand: and when they arose early in the morning, behold, they were all dead corpses. So Sennacherib king of Assyria departed, and went and returned, and dwelt at Nineveh."

Hezekiah made a serious error in not depending on God for direction and it would have ended in complete destruction if God had not intervened. God's blessings are available to all who ask for His grace and endless love.

2 Kings 20:1-6 reads, "In those days was Hezekiah sick unto death. And the prophet Isaiah the son of Amoz came to him, and said unto him, Thus saith the Lord, Set thine house in order; for thou shalt die, and not live. Then he turned has face to the wall, and prayed unto the Lord saying, I beseech thee, O Lord, remember now how I have walked before thee in truth and with a perfect heart, and have done that which is good in thy sight. And Hezekiah wept sore. And it came to pass, afore Isaiah was gone out into the middle court, that the word of the Lord came to him, saying, Turn again, and tell Hezekiah the captain of my people, Thus saith the Lord, the God of David thy father, I have heard thy prayer, I have seen thy tears: behold, I will heal thee: on the third day thou shalt go up unto the house of the Lord. And I will add unto thy days fifteen years; and I will deliver thee and this city out of the hand of the king of Assyria; and I will defend this city for mine own sake, and for my servant David's sake."

God was faithful to His word and He would protect David's line to the coming of the Messiah, Jesus Christ. Hezekiah was a godly man that had devoted his life to the worship of the one true God. God recognized Hezekiah's devotion and responded to His prayers for protection and added life. God answers prayers for those who are devoted, obey His commands, and live a righteous life.

APPLICATION

Hezekiah was a godly king who began his reign at the age of 25 and ruled over Judah for twenty-nine years. He had a close relationship with God and was considered to be one that did what was good and faithful before the Lord.

Unfortunately, like many others, pride became an issue and he endangered Judah by displaying all of the temple's gold to the Assyrians. Isaiah rebuked Hezekiah for this pride and poor judgment.

Hezekiah was considered a faithful king who placed his trust in God and was blessed with answered prayers that defeated the Assyrian army. Hezekiah in complete humility and obedience prayed to God throughout each day. He understood the power of prayer and realized he needed to communicate with God in order for God to develop within him a character that would be pleasing to God.

A man's soul and spirit were created by God for the purpose of communicating and communing with God. However, a man who is a non-believer can be spiritually dead. Consequently, the spirit of the believer connects with God and needs to be nourished by continual prayer and the Holy Spirit.

1 Timothy 4:8 reads, "For bodily exercise profiteth little: but godliness is profitable unto all things, having promise of the life that now is, and of that which is to come."

The importance of prayer cannot be overstated, since prayer has unlimited value in bringing blessings now and for all eternity. Man also needs to pray for spiritual strength to withstand the many temptations of Satan's attacks on a daily basis. The fall of man created a massive spiritual crevice between God and man that can only be crossed by believers in prayer. Man's fallen nature does not want to worship God and will create endless reasons and excuses not to worship God.

We spend our lives focusing on the world and its many distractions. We will spend years honing our skills and spend a great deal of money educating our selves to perform specific functions within society. At the same time most people spend little or no time on building a relationship with their Lord and Creator. The soul and spirit of man is the most important aspect of man and will last for eternity. Man's first priority needs to be to nurture the soul and spirit by developing a close relationship with God our Creator. Through the Holy Spirit this relationship grows and man will receive many blessings as God reveals His plan for each person's life.

God is a loving, merciful, omnipresent, omniscient, and omnipotent God. Man is not able to comprehend the depth and width of God's love and presence in the universe.

John 4:24 reads, "God is a Spirit: and they that worship him must worship him in spirit and in truth."

As a Spirit, God is able to know the thoughts and words of all men throughout the entire world and for all eternity. No matter where we are or the situation God is always there for our comfort and assurance. Man's spirit is limited and is contained within his body until death.

Ephesians 6:18, reads, "Praying always with all prayer and supplication in the Spirit, and watching thereunto with all perseverance and supplication for all saints."

Prayers need to be continual, thorough, and persistent. A prayer is spiritual in nature and each prayer is like a thread that ties man's spirit to God's Spirit. Over time a believer is able to grow spiritually and his prayers are weaved together like a strong rope that ties God's Spirit to the believer's spirit. The spiritual connection between man and God is the most beloved treasure man carries with Him for all eternity.

God throughout history has been communicating with man through His creation, commandments, laws, and prophets. God through Jesus came to this world for the purpose of instructing man how to live a Christ-like life. Jesus spent a great deal of time in prayer and taught man how to prayer. Our prayers are messages of love to God with our whole heart and mind. We pray in complete humility asking always for God's love and His will for our daily life.

Manasseh and Meshullemeth
Approximately (709—642 BC)

KING MANASSEH WAS A king that did not follow the godly example of his father Hezekiah. He began his reign at the age of 12 and ruled over Judah for 55 years. His rule included a co-reign with his father for about 10 years. This was one of the longest rules by a King of Judah and was viewed as evil by God.

2 Kings 21:2-3 reads, "And he did that which was evil in the sight of the Lord, after the abominations of the heathen, whom the Lord cast out before the children of Israel. For he built up again the high places which Hezekiah his father had destroyed; and he reared up alters for Baal, and made a grove, as did Ahab king of Israel; and worshiped all the host of heaven, and served them."

King Manasseh reversed many of his father's commands and efforts to bring the people back to worship of the one true God. It is believed that King Manasseh developed a trade relationship with the Assyrians and others that were deeply involved in pagan worship and many other pagan practices.

2 Chronicles 33:10-13 reads, "And the Lord spake to Manasseh, and to his people: but they would not hearken. Wherefore the Lord brought upon them the captains of the host of the king of Assyria, which took Manasseh among the thorns, and bound him with fetters, and carried him to Babylon. And when he was in affliction, he besought the Lord his God, and humbled himself greatly before the God of his fathers, And prayed unto him: and he was entreated of him, and heard his supplication, and brought him again to Jerusalem into his kingdom. Then Manasseh knew that the Lord he was God."

King Manasseh was a tragic figure in that he could not correct all the damage he had created with the worship of idols and pagan gods. God loves us, but He cannot tolerate evil or sin. Nothing can be hidden from God and all sin (big and small) will be exposed and we all must give account for all our sins.

Isaiah 59:2 reads, "But your iniquities have separated between you and your God, and your sins have hid his face from you, that he will not hear."

Psalm 94:12 reads, "Blessed is the man whom thou chastenest, O Lord, and teachest him out of thy law."

Man's faith in his Lord and Savior allows entry into a relationship with God and a life everlasting.

APPLICATION

The world is desperately wicked and full of evil. Man is in a fallen state and Satan has placed him in a fog where spiritual truths cannot be seen and understood. We see the anger and hatred of man on a daily basis as men attack and kill each other for little or no reason. As we see more and more uncontrolled slaughter of innocence it makes the denial of the existence of Satan more and more difficult.

King Manasseh was also deeply involved in idol worship and in the slaughter of the innocence.

2 Kings 21:16 reads, "Moreover Manasseh shed innocent blood very much, till he had filled Jerusalem from one end to another; beside his sins wherewith he made Judah to sin, in doing that which was evil in the sight of the Lord."

King Manasseh had actually sacrificed his own son in following the practices of worshiping the pagan gods. God allowed King Manasseh to be captured by Assyria and be taken away for imprisonment. During his imprisonment King Manasseh realized he had lost everything and needed to ask forgiveness for his many sins. God in His grace allowed King Manasseh to return to Judah as King for the remainder of his life. During these years he tried to reverse all the damage he had inflicted upon the people of Judah by removing all the idols and protecting the people from false religions.

1 Peter 2:11 reads, "Dearly beloved, I beseech you as strangers and pilgrims, abstain from fleshly lusts, which war against the soul:"

As Christians we live in a world that is not our home. We are to run from the lust of the world, immorality, and all the sinful desires of this world. Christians and their spiritual well-being are in a battle with Satan and his many followers. Satan and his warriors are in a search and destroy mission by continually confronting Christian's souls with fleshly lusts.

1 John 2:15-16 reads, "Love not the world, ether the things that are in the world. If any man love the world, the love of the Father is not in him. For all that is in the world, the lust of the flesh, and the lust of the eyes, and pride of life, is not of the Father, but is of the world."

Men work in many cases just to fulfill their desires of material things. They are basically fulfilling their vanity and love of self. Christians that are involved in these lusts need to change their lives, fall on their faces, and ask for forgiveness.

Man's worship of idols has and will always result in acts of wickedness and evil. Today churches are under attack by Satan and a society that demands that they adopt other translations of scripture in an effort to include those who worship self and live in sin.

Amon and Jedidah
Approximately (664–641 BC)

IT IS BELIEVED THAT King Amon began his reign at the age of 22 and ruled for only two years. He was assassinated in his palace by his own officials. Consequently, his son Josiah became ruler at the age of 8 years old.

2 Kings 21: 18-20 reads, "And Manasseh slept with his fathers, and was buried in the garden of his own house, in the garden of Uzza: and Amon his son reigned in his stead. Amon was twenty and two years old when he began to reign, and he reigned two years in Jerusalem. And his mother's name was Meshullemeth, the daughter of Haruz of Jotah. And he did that which was evil in the sight of the Lord, as his father Manasseh did."

King Amon supported the worship of pagan gods and all the other evil practices associated with pagan gods. Unfortunately, he never repented of his evil ways unlike his father, King Manasseh.

Isaiah 1:18-19 reads, "Come now, and let us reason together, saith the Lord: thought your sins be as a scarlet, they shall be as white as snow; though they be red like crimson, they shall be as wool. If ye be willing and obedient, ye shall eat the good of the land:"

God's gracious invitation is to all mankind. If man will repent of his sin he will experience the life changing grace of God. God stands ready and willing to cleanse and forgive all who will trust and obey Him.

APPLICATION

King Amon worshiped the pagan gods and God ended his rule after two years. It is difficult to understand why King Amon did not learn from the mistakes made by his father King Manasseh. It is believed there was a great deal of pressure from those who benefited financially from the sacrifices made to the pagan gods and other related pagan businesses and practices. In some ways the corrupt business practices of today may be similar to those during that time in history.

Another issue that needs to be addressed is the Promised Land and the people that lived in this land before being occupied by the Hebrews. The land was extremely fertile and had long been cared for by people that worship pagan gods and had never heard of the God of the Hebrews. Some of Israelites reasoned that the land was fertile because of the pagan gods and that they would continue the worship of pagan gods. This superstition and mythology continued for years as people struggled with good harvests in some years and years of famine. God continued to discipline the Hebrews for years as they failed and would later repent of their sins and return to the worship of the one true God.

This struggle continues today as people fail and are entrapped by their worship of wealth, possessions, pleasure and self.

Exodus 20:3-5 reads, "Thou shalt have no other gods before me. Thou shalt not make unto thee any graven image, or any likeness of any thing that is in heaven above, or that is in the earth beneath, or that is in the water under the earth. Thou shalt not bow down thyself to them, nor serve them: for I the Lord thy God am a jealous God, visiting the iniquity of the fathers upon the children unto the third and fourth generation of them that hate me;"

Today, people worship many different types of idols or false gods. Many people are addicted to gambling, drugs and will steal and kill in order to gamble more and purchase more drugs. Some people will spend their entire life hunting for the right house, car, clothes, and many other material and non material things. Today, there seems to be an endless list of things people worship. People today are like sheep that will follow without question the values and morals of the world.

Some humans are highly intelligent and have been able to make important progress in improving the lives of people all over the world. Men take great pride in these accomplishments and generally give little or no recognition to God and His blessings of grace. In fact, in many cases men will use these great strides for mankind as opportunities to worship themselves and discredit the idea that God was connected in any way. Throughout history man has worked at trying to discredit God and the idea that He created the universe. In some respects, it seems almost humorous since the life span of a man is almost nonexistent compared to eternity and God the Creator of all things.

God created man with a mind that is capable of resolving complex problems, building massive beautiful buildings, composing wonderful music, and painting and creating magnificent works of art. Man is able to consider many ideas and make judgments based on reason and his understanding of the world and his experiences. Man is also able to experience and express emotions in any number of ways for any number of reasons.

The world and evil would like all men believe that this magnificent human being is simply a product of evolution and random selection. No reasonable person would believe this distressing theory that man pulled himself out of a pool of slim and grew to this magnificent human capable of reflecting God's image and grace. But, yet the text books for the youth of this country and the world are filled with the theory of evolution and other distressing ideas.

This is surely one of the most offensive and disgusting ideas that has confronted God. Knowing how God has disciplined the Israelites for their sins, this is certainly going to provoke the wrath of God in many different ways.

Man understands little about how the brain of man operates and absolutely nothing about the soul and spirit, the most important parts of man.

King Amon was included in the Messiah bloodline and represented the sin of mankind and the evil that permeates men's life on earth.

Josiah and Hamutal
Approximately (648–609 BC)

KING JOSIAH AT THE age of eight was the youngest recorded king. Josiah grew to be a king that walked with his Lord and kept His commandments and laws. The king wanted to please God, he had all idols removed from the land, and repaired the temple.

2 Kings 22: 1-2 reads, "Josiah was eight years old when he began to reign, and he reigned thirty and one years in Jerusalem. And his mother's name was Jedidah, the daughter of Adaiah of Boscath. And he did that which was right in the sight of the Lord, and walked in all the way of David his father, and returned not aside to the right hand or the left."

2 Kings 23:25 reads, "And like unto him was there no king before him, that turned to the Lord with all his heart, and with all his soul, and with all his might, according to all the law of Moses; neither after him arose there any like him."

King Josiah was a great king that followed all the laws and commandments of God.

2 Kings 22:19 reads, "Because thine heart was tender, and thou hast humbled thyself before the Lord, when thou heardest what I spake against this place, and against the inhabitants thereof, that they should become a desolation and a curse, and hast rent thy clothes, and wept before me; I also have heard thee, saith the Lord."

Josiah lived a life that was fully committed to the Lord and obedient to God and he was blessed because of it. If your heart is responsive to the Lord and you humble yourself before Him, He will hear your prayer. Josiah did die in a battle against the Egyptians and was buried in Jerusalem. His son Jechoniah took the reign as king after his death. Jechoniah's mother was Hamutal.

Matthew 1:11 reads, "And Josiah begot Jechoniah and his brethren, about the time they were carried away to Babylon."

APPLICATION

King Josiah was a child that had the heart for the Lord and His commandments. Jesus instructed his disciples that they needed to become like children in order to enter the kingdom of God. As a child is completely dependent on a parent a man needs to become dependent on God.

Luke 9:46-48 reads, "Then there arose a reasoning among them, which of them should be greatest. And Jesus, perceiving the thought of their heart, took a child, and set him by him. And said unto them, Whosoever shall receive this child in my name receiveth me: and whosoever shall receive me receiveth him that sent me: for he that is least among you all, the same shall be great."

God is looking for those who are humble, trusting, and open to instruction. A child is completely dependent on the parent for his daily needs just as a believer is completely dependent of God to provide for his daily needs. A believer realizes that his life is but a whisper in time and that he needs to place all his trust in God.

Idols are formed by man on a daily basis as he makes decisions between trusting in God for His direction or trusting in man's wisdom. No decision should be made without first requesting God's help and His will. The point is that God is always recognized first in all decisions and has our complete devotion.

Philippians 4:6 reads, "Be careful for noting; but in every thing by prayer and supplication with thanksgiving let your requests be made known unto God."

We should be sharing all of our issues and thoughts with God on a daily basis. Each day is made of many different issues that when combined can amount to a serious trend that requires our attention. Our prayers should be made with all humility and our requests should be made with heartfelt desire for God's protection and His will to be completed in our lives.

Babylonian Exile
Approximately (608–538BC)

THE DEPORTATION AND EXILE of the Jewish people from Judah was an effective method for controlling a newly conquered land. In addition, people from other lands immigrated to the newly conquered Judah to maintain existing crop production and other infrastructure needs. The dates and number of people that were deported from Judah to other locations varies. It is believed that the exile lasted 70 years and that the Jewish people immigrated back to Judah over many years.

Jeremiah 29:10 reads, "For thus saith the Lord, That after seventy years be accomplished at Babylon I will visit you, and perform my good word toward you, in causing you to return to this place."

The Babylonian army captured Jerusalem and carried away all of its treasures and all those who were related to the king. All those that were in the Judah army and all the skilled craftsmen were forced to relocate to Babylon.

Jechoniah and wife unknown
Approximately (615–562BC)

IT IS BELIEVED THAT King Jechoniah was also called Jeconiah, Jechonias, Jehoiachin, and Coniah. The entire region during this time period was experiencing a great deal of turmoil and many people were forced to relocate to other areas within the Mediterranean region.

King Jechoniah listened to the spiritualists and those that claimed to know the future. He refused to listen to the prophet Jeremiah and did not pay tribute to the king of Babylon that resulted in God allowing the Babylonian army to capture Jerusalem and all of Judah.

Jeremiah 27:9-11 reads, "Therefore hearken not ye to your prophets, nor to your diviners, nor to your dreamers, nor to your enchanters, nor to your sorcerers, which speak unto you saying, Ye shall not serve the king of Babylon. For they prophesy a lie unto you, to remove you far from your land; and that I should drive you out, and ye should perish. But the nations that bring their neck under the yoke of the king of Babylon, and serve him, those will I let remain still in their own land, saith the Lord; and they shall till it, and dwell therein."

King Jechoniah refused to listen to Jeremiah the prophet and he and the people of Jerusalem suffered the consequences.

King Jechoniah was king for only a few months before he was captured by the Babylon army and King Nebuchadnezzar. King Jechoniah and those that were related to him and reported to him were all relocated and imprisoned in Babylon for many years while Nebuchadnezzar was in power.

2 kings 24:8 reads, "Jehoiachin was eighteen years old when he began to reign, and he reigned in Jerusalem three months. And his mother's name was Nehushta, the daughter of Elnathan of Jerusalem. And he did that which was evil in the sight of the Lord, according to all that his father had

done. At that time the servants of Nebuchadnezzar king of Babylon came up against Jerusalem, and the city was besieged. And Nebuchadnezzar king of Babylon came against the city and his servants did besiege it."

APPLICATION

Jeremiah was born in a small city just north of Jerusalem about 627 B.C. He was fearless in denouncing the idol worship of the people and those who were in leadership. Jeremiah spoke as God's prophet to King Jechoniah for the purpose of conveying God's purpose and the leading for the people of Judah.

Deuteronomy 18:18-19 reads, "I will raise them up a Prophet from among their brethren, like unto thee, and will put my words in his mouth; and he shall speak unto them all that I shall command him. And it shall come to pass, that whosoever will not hearken unto my words which he shall speak my name, I will require it if him."

It was not uncommon for God to use prophets to deliver His message of faith to His people. God spoke to the people of Judah through the prophet Jeremiah. Jeremiah spent a great deal of his time trying to make the people of Judah realize that they needed to place their trust and faith in the one true God. They had failed once again and had fallen back to the worship of gods from Egypt.

Jeremiah 9:23-24 reads, "Thus saith the Lord, Let not the wise man glory in his wisdom, neither let the mighty man glory in his might, let not the rich man glory in his riches: But let him that glorieth glory in this, that he understandeth and knoweth me, that I am the Lord which exercise loving kindness, judgment, and righteousness, in the earth: for in these things I delight, saith the Lord."

Jeremiah reminds the people of Judah that true wisdom comes from God and not from self or the worship of idols. Only God provides true wisdom and that wisdom is based on the loving kindness of God, a true and consistent provider of judgment, and righteousness of a true and loving God.

Jeremiah 17: 9-10 reads, "The heart is deceitful above all things, and desperately wicked: who can know it? I the Lord search the heart, I try the reins, even to give every man according to his ways, and according to the fruit of his doings."

The heart of the fallen man is deceitful and is naturally sinful. It is only God's grace that allows a believer to commune with his Savior. Therefore it is only God that knows man's motives and innermost thoughts. Consequently, it is only God who can judge the heart and determine what discipline is required.

It was only God who could create a bridge that would allow fallen man an avenue to salvation.

1 Corinthians 1:31 reads, "That, according as it is written, He that glorieth, let him glory in the Lord."

It was Christ and His death that allowed man the opportunity to grow into righteousness and holiness. It was through the redemption of Christ the Lord that allowed God's grace to be delivered to all of mankind.

Today we have the complete revelation from God in the Bible. In the past God used prophets to build the foundation for the early church. However, today God does work through individuals to deliver inspired messages based on the Bible. We need to be aware and to test any new idea against God's inspired word the Bible.

2 Timothy 3:16 reads, "All scripture is given by inspiration of God, and is profitable for doctrine, for reproof, for correction, for instruction in righteousness:"

Salathiel and wife unknown
Approximately (586–540 BC)

THERE IS AN ISSUE with the father of Salathiel between the Gospel of Matthew and Luke. For the purpose of this book all genealogy references are consistently based on the gospel of Matthew.

King Salathiel like the rest of the royal family during this time period was exiled to Babylon. There is little known about King Salathiel and his activities during this time period.

APPLICATION

Again, we see another example of God disciplining the Hebrews for their idol worship and disobedience to God's word with the exile of the people of Judah to Babylon.

We need always to be aware of God's commandments and live a life that is in compliance with His word so that we may experience His loving blessings instead of His loving discipline. Like the Jewish people of Judah God provides a path back from sin and that path is faith and trust in the Lord, God Almighty.

Galatians 1:3-4 reads, "Grace be to you and peace from God the Father, and from our Lord Jesus Christ. Who gave himself for our sins, that he might deliver us from this evil world, according to the will of God and our Father:"

Today the moral and spiritual environment of this world is rapidly deteriorating. Satan is applying greater pressure on the Christian church to conform to his standards and accept morals that are completely against the scripture. Those churches that refuse to accept these immoral standards will experience persecution from society.

Society is returning to the pagan values of the past where all beliefs are acceptable and a greater rejection of those churches that hold fast to the spiritual truths of the Bible. It will be only those churches that hold fast to the Holy Scripture that will be able to withstand Satan's attacks and experience the power of God. Many churches will collapse under the pressure of Satan and conform to the world's values in an attempt to survive.

Satan lives in the spiritual realm of our lives and is able to inflict great pain if allowed by God. He is extremely powerful; however his power is limited and is subject to God's rule.

1 Peter 5:8 reads, "Be sober, be vigilant; because your adversary the devil, as a roaring lion, walketh about, seeking whom he may devour."

Satan cannot be under estimated because he is extremely clever and knows no limit in overwhelming a believer with persecution and trying to break his communion with God. It is extremely important that the believer maintain a strong faith, following God's word and obeying his commandments.

Zerubbabel and Esthra
Approximately (566–510 BC)

THE DEATH OF THE Babylon King Nebuchadnezzar and the invasion by Cyrus the Great of Persia resulted in the release of the Jewish people from Babylon. Cyrus the Great was a respecter of religion of the land which resulted in a positive impact on the Jewish people.

Zerubbabel with the title governor was allowed to lead the Jewish people in returning to Judah and Jerusalem. It was Zerubbabel that lead in the rebuilding of the temple in Jerusalem and the carrying on of the line of David.

Haggai 2:23 reads, "In that day, saith the Lord of hosts, will I take thee, O Zerubbabel, my servant, the son of Shealtiel, saith the Lord, and will make thee as a signet: for I have chosen thee, saith he Lord of hosts."

Zerubbabel stood as an official representative of the Davidic line and the arrival of Jesus Christ the Messiah. It was God that directed Zerubbabel in the building of the second temple.

Zechariah 4:5-7 reads, "Then the angel that talked with me answered and said unto me, Knowest thou not what these be? And I said, No, my lord. Then he answered and spake unto me, saying, This is the word of the Lord unto Zerubbabel, saying, Not by might, nor by power, but by my spirit, saith the Lord of hosts. Who art thou, O great mountain? before Zerubbabel thou shall become a plain: and he shall bring forth the headstone thereof with shouting, crying, Grace, grace unto it."

God through the Holy Spirit designed and protected the building of the temple and did eliminate all obstacles that would have prevented the completion of the temple. God working through Zerubbabel provided the direction and leadership that made the rebuilding of the temple possible.

We need to remember that God has a plan and that we are a part of that plan. We also need to remember that the Holy Spirit can eliminate any obstacle, provide direction when needed, and empower us to complete His will.

APPLICATION

Each person has free will and has the opportunity to decide to believe in God's saving grace through Jesus Christ or not to believe in God and the sacrifice of His Son, Jesus Christ. Those that decide to believe and accept God's free gift of salvation will become part of God's perfect plan. Their lives will take on new meaning and God will use them for His purpose in His perfect plan.

Jeremiah 29:11 reads, "For I know the thoughts that I think toward you, saith the Lord, thoughts of peace, and not of evil, to give you an expected end."

God's plan would bring peace to the Hebrew people and would bring them back to Judah after many years of exile to Babylon. The exile of God's people caused them to realize they needed to worship the one true God. At that point, God collected His people from Babylon and other lands and return them to the Promised Land. At that point, God used King Zerubbabel to reconstruct Jerusalem and the temple.

We need to pay attention to the current circumstance and see if God is allowing new opportunities for new ministries. It is during prayer that God will speak to us as to what actions should be taken, what needs to be repaired, and what areas need additional work. As Christians we have all surrendered our wills to God and have placed our complete trust in Him for direction in living a more obedient life.

God has created each of us with specific talents to be used for His purpose and plan. In fact, God's will for each believer is revealed in God's Holy Scriptures and begins with obeying His commandments. Obedience to God's commandments is the first step that needs to be taken before more of God's will is unfolded for our lives. Obedience can be difficult for some Christians because of the pressures inflicted by the world and weakness of the fallen man to always think in terms of self and how the ego is impacted.

The believer experiences the guidance of the Holy Spirit when meditating on God's Holy Scriptures. It is the studying and praying over the Bible that allows the Holy Spirit to flood man's spirit with many new ideas and feelings. The Holy Spirit at times may bring great joy, peace, and comfort. And at other times the Holy Spirit may bring great sadness, conviction, and guilt over missed opportunities.

John 10:27 reads,"My sheep hear my voice, and I know them, and they follow me."

The Christian is locked into eternal security and can never be separated from God's love. It is the Christian that believes and trusts that the Son the God humbled himself to be the sacrifice to deliver all believers from the heavy burden of sin.

Abiud and Tamita
Approximately (475– 400BC)

THE NAME ABIUD IS only mentioned once in the Bible. The name Abiud is listed in the genealogy listed in the Gospel of Matthew.

The genealogy of a family was an integral part of Jewish society and was used to determine how land was inherited from generation to generation. Jesus was able to trace His genealogy back to the first man, Adam. Therefore, the life of Jesus and His death allowed the sin of Adam and all of mankind to be forgiven. Messiah was able to tie the sin of the first man to the forgiveness of all sin by the Savior of all men, Jesus Christ.

Romans 5:18 reads, "Therefore as by the offense of one judgment came upon all me to condemnation; even so by the righteousness of one the free gift came upon all men into justification of life."

Throughout all of history and the Old Testament a Savior was promised to take away man's burden of sin. The Apostle Matthew with God's direction recorded the genealogy of Jesus the Christ as a descendant of Abraham, Isaac, Jacob, and David.

APPLICATION

We know little about the Abiud listed in the Gospel of Mathew. However, God created His church from millions of unknown people over thousands of years that worshiped the one true God. These millions of unknown believers experienced persecution in many different forms, from reputations being destroyed to crucifixion. For example, those who refused to pay homage to a pagan god a penalty of death could be inflicted. These unknown believers also struggled against many different evil kings, rulers, beliefs, and religious leaders. The fact that many early Christians were willing to die for their beliefs has had a lasting impact on the survival of the church.

John 15:20-21 reads, "Remember the word that I said unto you, The servant is not greater than his lord. If they have persecuted me, they will also persecute you; if they have kept my saying, they will keep yours also. But all these things will they do unto you for my name's sake, because they know not him that sent me."

As Christians we need to enter our churches in complete humility with a profound appreciation of all the millions of unknown believers who in many cases freely gave their lives so that we may worship in God's house. Christianity offers new hope and clarity to a world filled with chaos, fear, and brutality. Christianity is kind and longsuffering and provides a sense of family where in many cases families have been destroyed by greed and the worship of self.

Eliakim and wife unknown
Approximately (455–392 BC)

THE NAME ELIAKIM IS listed in a number of different places in the Bible. However, the Eliakim listed in the Gospel of Matthew and Luke is believed to be a different person.

The Jewish people were not looking for a descendant of David and an unknown humble person from Nazareth. The Jewish people were looking for their Messiah to be a great king of war who would bring judgment upon evil doers. Their king would bring a great war between good and evil.

Zechariah 9: 9 reads, "Rejoice greatly, O daughter of Zion; shout, O daughter of Jerusalem: behold, thy King cometh unto thee: he is just, and having salvation; lowly, and riding upon an ass, and upon a colt the foal of an ass."

Jesus came as Lord of Lords and King of Kings, a man of great love and justice, and a humble servant. Jesus made the ultimate sacrifice and paid the price for our sins to be forgiven.

APPLICATION

The Apostle Matthew listed Eliakim as another unknown name in the bloodline for the Messiah. The Jewish people were looking for the Messiah to be a mighty king that would destroy all the enemies of the Jewish people and all sinners both Jew and Gentile.

The Jewish people suffered for many years as they moved to Egypt, lived as slaves under the Pharaoh's rule, wandered in the desert, fought and captured the Promised Land, lived under the rule of evil Kings, and were tortured and publicly crucified under Roman rule. The Jewish people were subject to the corruption of the tax collector and the temple priests. They were looking for a war-like king that would publicly judge and destroy their enemies and establish a kingdom to rule the entire world.

Jesus did not come as an earthly king but as Savior of all sinners. Jesus was offering forgiveness to all sinners who would believe on His name. The message was clear that we are all sinners and that all men are in need of forgiveness for their sins. God's message is a message of love. God is a loving, long suffering, patience God who is willing to forgive all of mankind for all of their sins.

Zechariah 9:9 reads, "Rejoice greatly, O daughter of Zion; shout, O daughter of Jerusalem: behold, thy King cometh unto thee: he is just, and having salvation; lowly, and riding upon an ass, and upon a colt the foal of an ass."

This prophecy was fulfilled when Jesus entered the gates of the city Jerusalem. Jesus is described as a man who is a king; humble, just, and brings salvation.

John 12:12-16 reads, "On the next day much people that were come to the feast, when they heard that Jesus was coming to Jerusalem, Took branches of palm trees, and went forth to meet him, and cried, Hosanna: Blessed is the King of Israel that cometh in the name of the Lord. And Jesus, when he had found a young ass, sat thereon, as it is written. Fear not daughter of Zion: Behold, Thy King cometh, sitting on an ass's colt. These things understood not his disciples at the first: but when Jesus was glorified, then remembered they that these things were written of him, and that they had done these things unto him."

The people of Israel were shouting Hosanna and waving palms for the purpose of recognizing Jesus as the Messiah and the Son of God. Many people had seen or were aware of Jesus' many miracles and had come to praise the name of Jesus as the Messiah.

Azor and wife unknown
Approximately (435–341 BC)

THE NAME AZOR APPEARS only once in the Bible as part of the genealogy of Jesus within the Gospel of Matthew. The fact that this name only appears once does not in any way minimize the importance of the name Azor. This person was part of God's plan to bring the Savior of the world to this earth. Azor carried the bloodline that would give all of mankind the opportunity to believe in a God that offers eternal life. This simple act of placing your faith in God opens the doors to the Holy Spirit to come into your daily life.

We pray that God's will would be made complete in our daily lives and that we would experience His grace and love throughout each day. There are millions of unknown people who have an equally important part in fulfilling God's plan for all of our lives.

APPLICATION

God uses unknown people throughout our lives to guide and direct us throughout our lives. In some cases we are aware how God uses others and in some situations we will only understand when we meet them in heaven. Unknown people may at times be responsible for pain or pleasure in our life. The effects of these encounters may be lessened or altered by our prayers and God's will.

The Jewish people were continually caught in a cycle of disobedience, discipline, repentance, and blessings. The reason was due to a number of issues related to their fallen nature, self-love, pagan gods, and Satan's influences. We should not be surprised if God disciplines us for our disobedience. He is a gracious loving God who continually guides and directs our actions on a daily basis. Just as a loving parent, God will use a number of different methods and others to influence our words, thoughts, and actions on a daily basis.

Christians are guided and directed by the Holy Spirit on a daily basis. God has created each of us, His Spirit dwells within us, and He loves us all unconditionally. We are not alone as God's Spirit ministers to each of us each day in many different ways. We grow in our Christian faith as the Holy Spirit ministers to us through others as they share their different experiences, perspectives, and gifts.

John 14: 16-17 reads, "And I will pray the Father, and he shall give you another Comforter, that he may abide with you for ever; Even the Spirit of truth; whom the world cannot receive, because it seeth him not, neither knoweth him: but ye know him; for he dwelleth with you, and shall be in you."

Today, Christians find comfort in the Holy Spirit and are able to rely on Him for peace and comfort in difficult times. It is important that we surround ourselves with other Christians for encouragement, grow in understanding of others experiences, and grow in appreciation and humility for God's grace and love for imperfect people.

Sadoc and Kaltimi
Approximately (320–270 BC)

SADOC WAS A DESCENDANT of Zerubbabel and ancestor of the Messiah, Jesus Christ. Sadoc is an unknown name that is only mentioned in the genealogy found in the Gospel of Matthew. This book consistently refers to the King James and the Gospel of Matthew and uses the exact references and spelling found in the King James. Sadoc is spelled Zadok in the NIV. It is not uncommon for names to have different spellings due to different translations and other reasons. Another challenge is that the same name may be used by different people.

The Apostle Matthew was a highly intelligent and gifted man who wrote this gospel under the direction of the Holy Spirit. Consequently, this gospel and any reference to the Bible has been taken as God's inerrant word and has not been changed in any way. There is no discussion or opinion given as to why certain kings were not mentioned by the Apostle Matthew. Again, the Bible is the inerrant word of God and needs to be read with our human ability to understand and apply to our daily lives.

APPLICATION

The name Sadoc was believed to mean a righteous man that was honest, just, and lawful. This person would have worshiped the one true God and would have not worshiped the idols of the land. However, all men sin and therefore cannot be perfect and be called righteous.

Jesus was the only man to live a sin free righteous life. Consequently, it is impossible for man to live a sin free life and achieve righteousness through obedience. We are all guilty of sin and would spend eternity in hell if it wasn't for God's grace that paid the penalty for our sins. God came in the person of Jesus Christ to pay the price for all of mankind's sin. Man can only be justified and forgiven of his sins when he believes in the crucifixion and resurrection of Jesus Christ.

Romans:3:23-26 reads, "For all have sinned, and come short of the glory of God; Being justified freely by his grace through the redemption that is in Christ Jesus: Whom God hath set forth to be a propitiation through faith in his blood, to declare his righteousness for the remission of sins that are past, through the forbearance of God; To declare, I say, at this time his righteousness: that he might be just, and the justifier of him which believeth in Jesus."

The Apostle Paul in this verse was describing the vast never ending holiness of God. God is the same today, yesterday and forever. God is holy, righteous, just, patience, loving, and is ever present in our daily lives. God's sacrifice of His only Son declared His righteousness in the forgiveness of all of mankind's sins, past, present and future. It is only by God's grace through faith that man is able to avoid God's wrath and the penalty for man's sin.

Achim and Asbaoda
Approximately (300– 250 BC)

ACHIM MAY BE A name that is unique to Joseph's family and may not have appeared in the Old Testament. There are millions of unknown Christians that have made monumental contributions to God's plan for all of mankind.

Matthew 25:23 reads, " His Lord said unto him, Well done, good and faithful servant , thou hast been faithful over a few things , I will make thee ruler over many things: enter thou into the joy of thy Lord."

We are all given unique talents that are to be faithfully used to further the gospel of our Lord and Master. Our faith is reflected in our consistent faithfulness and in how we use these God-given talents on a daily basis.

APPLICATION

A faithful servant for God is one that controls his desires for the world and is able to place worship as his first priority. Having a servant's attitude is difficult because it requires placing yourself under the leadership and direction of another. It is placing your trust in another for fair treatment, payment for services rendered, and appreciation for a job well done.

2 Timothy 4:7-8 reads, "I have fought a good fight, I have finished my course, I have kept the faith: Henceforth there is laid up for me a crown of righteousness, which the lord, the righteous judges, shall give me at that day: and not to me only, but unto all them also that love his appearing."

As Christians we are to be fully engaged in presenting the gospel to all that will hear. This is our reasonable service as a follower and servant of Jesus Christ. God has been a faithful servant to all of mankind for thousands of generations.

Deuteronomy 7:9 reads, "Know therefore that the Lord thy God, he is God, the faithful God which keepeth covenant and mercy with them that love him and keep his commandments to a thousand generations;"

God will never abandon those that love Him and keep His commandments.

Eliud and wife unknown
Approximately (160– 100BC)

THE NAME ELIUD IS only mentioned once in the Gospel of Matthew as an ancestor of Jesus Christ. Eliud was the great-great-great-grandfather by law of Jesus Christ. Jesus' teachings were focus on the fulfilling of the Israel and Jewish tradition of the law. Therefore, the Gospel of Matthew places great importance on showing that Jesus was the son of David and traces the genealogy back to Abraham.

Matthew 5:17-20 reads, "Think not that I am come to destroy the law, or the prophets: I am not come to destroy, but to fulfill. For verily I say unto you, Till heaven and earth pass, one jot or one tittle shall in no wise pass from the law, till all be fulfilled. Whosoever therefore shall break one of these commandments, and shall teach men so, he shall be called the least in the kingdom of heaven: but whosoever shall do and teach them, the same shall be called great in the kingdom of heaven. For I say unto you, That except your righteousness shall exceed the righteousness of all the scribes and Pharisees, ye shall in no case enter into the kingdom of heaven."

The importance of fulfilling the Old Testament cannot be understated. God's plan is perfect in every detail and the Apostle Matthew understood that fact. The life and ministry of Jesus was prophesied in a number of covenants in the Old Testament and fulfilled in the New Testament. Each and every promise made in Moses' law in the entire Old Testament was fulfilled.

Isaiah 9:6-7 reads, "For unto us a child is born, unto us a son is given: and the government shall be upon his shoulder: and his name shall be called Wonderful, Counselor, The mighty God, The everlasting Father , The Prince of Peace. Of the increase of his government and peace there shall be no end, upon the throne of David, and upon his kingdom, to order it, and to establish it with judgment and with justice from henceforth even and ever. The zeal of the Lord of hosts will perform this."

Isaiah the prophet was able to prophesy the arrival of God's perfect gift to all of mankind and that gift was Jesus Christ the Messiah. God Almighty through His infinite wisdom was able to provide mankind a path to salvation.

APPLICATION

The Messiah and His rule was prophesied when God promised David that his rule would be established forever.

2 Samuel 7:12-13 reads, "And when thy days be fulfilled, and thou shall sleep with thy fathers, I will set up thy seed after thee, which shall proceed out of thy bowels, and I will establish his kingdom. He shall build a house for my name, and I will establish the throne of his kingdom for ever."

From that point forward the Jewish people were looking for the one who would destroy their enemies, rule the land in God's name, and be from the family of David. The Jewish people misunderstood Jesus' mission and wanted him to be like King David and create a great kingdom in Israel. Man's fallen nature causes him to think in terms of his earthly condition and not of his soul and spirit. The Jewish people of the time did not understand Jesus' kingdom was not of this world and that they needed to trust in Jesus Christ as their heavenly Savior. Jesus was offering them eternal salvation not an earthly kingdom.

The Apostle John records the second coming in the Book of Revelations. Again, God is rejected by the people.

Revelations 11:17-18 reads, "Saying, We give thee thanks, O Lord God Almighty, which art, and wast, and art to come; because thou hast taken to thee thy great power, and hast reigned. And the nations were angry, and thy wrath is come, and the time of the dead, that they should be judged, and that thou shouldest give reward unto thy servants the prophets, and to the saints, and them that fear thy name, small and great: and shouldest destroy them which destroy the earth."

We will all fall on our faces as the Almighty God comes the second time to judge the nations, judge the dead, and to reward God's servants. We should not be surprised if people reject Christianity since man has rejected a belief in the one true God from the beginning.

Eleazar and Salome
Approximately (120– 50BC)

IT IS BELIEVED THAT Eleazar was the father of Matthan and married to Salome. There is little known about Eleazar and his family. There are millions of unknown Christians that have been martyred under the Roman Empire. Many Christians have died for their faith over the centuries. Their memorial is the existence of the church which has lasted for over two thousand years.

Rome worshiped many gods for fear of the wrath from these gods. Consequently, Romans were required to make scarifies to the gods at their Roman temples for fear of some type of disaster. Christians were viewed with distain because of their different beliefs and refusal to make sacrifices to Rome's pagan gods. Christians quickly became the target for many different types of persecutions and were blamed for Rome's burning and bringing other harm to the Roman Empire. For many years anyone confessing to be a Christian would be arrested, tortured and executed. Mass executions took place as jails became filled to capacity and Christians refused to recount their belief.

The harder the Romans tried to eliminate all Christians the stronger and faster faith grew throughout the Mediterranean area.

Romans 8:35 reads, "Who shall separate us from the love of Christ? shall tribulation, or distress, or persecution, or famine, or nakedness, or peril, or sword."

Roman 8:38-39 reads, "For I am persuaded, that neither death, nor life, nor angels, nor principalities, nor powers, nor things present, nor things to come. Nor height, nor depth, nor any other creature, shall be able to separate us from the love of God, which is in Christ Jesus our Lord."

APPLICATION

Man is dead in his sins that follow the values and pleasures of the world. He is disobedient to God's commands and lives for the passions of the flesh and acts out the desires of the mind and the failings of his nature. But God's grace opened the door to salvation to all who wish to break the chains of Satan and his power over their daily lives. There is nothing that can separate a Christian from the love of his Savior and Lord.

James 1:1-3 reads, "James, a servant of God and of the Lord Jesus Christ, to the twelve tribes, which are scattered abroad greeting. My brethren, count it all joy when ye fall into diverse temptations; Knowing this, that the trying of your faith worketh patience."

God through Jesus Christ will continue to guard and protect our hearts and our minds from trials and temptations by providing strength, peace, and perseverance.

A person today who decides to believe in Jesus Christ and His commandments will immediately receive the Holy Spirit into their life. From that point forward this person will be sealed for eternity and placed under God's spiritual protection. The Holy Spirit will grow within this person and provide this person with many spiritual gifts. The fruits of the Spirit are love, joy, peace, gentleness, goodness, perseverance, and faith.

As Christians we need to remember that we are in a spiritual battle with spiritual principalities, against powers, against rulers of the darkness, and wickedness. Consequently, we as Christians need to strengthen our Spirits with God's armor of truth, righteousness, peace, and the shield of faith, helmet of salvation, and the Spirit of God's word.

Matthan and Hazibah
Approximately (58–1BC)

THE NAME MATTHAN IS only mentioned once by Matthew in his genealogy found in Matt.1:15. The Gospel of Matthew begins with the genealogy of Christ and is a reflection of the beginning of the Book of Genesis. The Old Testament clearly reveals that God is completely in control and is the Creator of all history. God uses the Old Testament as a foundation for the revelation and salvation delivered by Jesus Christ in the New Testament.

The Jewish people under the rule of the Roman Empire for centuries were in many cases transported back to Rome as slaves. These Jewish slaves lived in desperation for many years practicing their religion in secret for fear of persecution. It is believed that both Peter and Paul in their missionary journeys were able to reach many of these enslaved people and bring them to the knowledge of Jesus the Christ and His message of salvation. These early unknown Christians lived out their lives under extreme persecution and in fear of execution.

Today the persecution of Christians still exists in many countries in the world. In some cases the persecution is sanctioned by governments such as Sudan where the population is almost entirely Muslim.

APPLICATION

We are all going to die. Many people die due to cancer, heart failure, accidents, and many other unforeseen deadly reasons. Jesus was asked by the disciples why a certain man was blind.

John 9:1-3 reads, "And as Jesus passed by, he saw a man which was blind from his birth. And his disciples asked him, saying, Master, who did sin, this man, or his parents, that he was born blind? Jesus answered,

Neither hath this man sinned, nor his parents: but that the works of God should be manifest to him."

Our task as Christians is to simply pray with faith. Our prayers are to be continual throughout each day, praising God's name, thanking God for His many blessings, asking for healing, and growing in strength and faith in a God that loves us without end. As we grow in faith our access and sensitivity to His Spirit also increases. Our trials are for the purpose of bringing us all to the same place in life and to the realization that we are all dependent on God for His love, peace, comfort, and healing. We all share the common experience of trials and are all able to pray for each other with a love, sorrow, empathy, and generosity of spirit.

James 1:6-7 reads, "But let him ask in faith, nothing waving. For he that wavereth is like a wave of the sea driven with the wind and tossed. For let not that man think that he shall receive any thing of the Lord."

A man who does not recognize God's power, trust in God's ability, or understands God's willingness to provide wisdom will be tossed about like a wave in the sea.

Hebrews 11:6 reads, "But without faith it is impossible to please him: for he that cometh to God must believe that he is, and that he is a rewarder of them that diligently seek him."

It is extremely important that we diligently seek God's will on a daily basis in all that we do and say. As we see God's will and plan unfold for our lives we grow in faith and we begin to adopt God's thoughts as our thoughts.

Romans 12:2 reads, "And be not conformed to this world: but be ye transformed by the renewing of your mind, that ye may prove what is that good, and acceptable , and prefect, will of God."

The world and it's values are controlled by Satan and his ability to dictate what is popular and acceptable to the common man. The world and Satan are able to influence the language they use, and what moral standards and values are acceptable. We see the most vulnerable in our society (the children) being slaughtered in their schools by those that are copying the violence they are taught by television and other media. Satan's purpose is for man to destroy himself by any means possible.

Jacob and Gadat
Approximately (40BC–20 AD)

THE GENEALOGY OF A family was extremely important at that time for the purpose of showing the rank, power and social status of a family in the community. The genealogy recorded by the Apostle Matthew of Jesus Christ the Messiah is extremely important for a number of reasons. First, it clearly documents how the prophecies of the Old Testament unfolded in the New Testament.

Jeremiah prophesied that one day God would raise up a king from the house of David that would provide both justice and judgment for all of the world.

Jeremiah 23:5-6 reads, "Behold, the days come, saith the Lord, that I will raise unto David a righteous Branch, and a king shall reign and prosper, and shall execute judgment and justice in the earth."

Jeremiah's prophecy was fulfilled when Jesus (a son of King David) declared His kingdom was not of this world, but was a kingdom in heaven.

John 18:36-37 reads, "Jesus answered, My kingdom is not of this world: if my kingdom were of this world, then would my servants fight, that I should not be delivered to the Jews: but now is my kingdom not from hense. Pilot therefore said unto him, Art thou a king then? Jesus answered, thou sayest that I am a king. To this end was I born, and for this cause came I into this world, that I should bear witness unto the truth. Every one that is of the truth hearth my voice."

The Son of Man's genealogy was a royal genealogy that fulfilled the Old Testament prophecy that the Messiah would be born in Bethlehem by a virgin birth, would be a son of David, would perform many miracles, die on the cross for all of man's sins, and rise from the grave on the third day defeating death and all of Satan's authority and powers.

APPLICATION

Abraham was faithful and obedient to God's direction and moved to Canaan. There God's plan for the nation of Israel would unfold and the descendants of Abraham would be blessed.

Genesis 12:1-3 reads, "Now the Lord had said unto Abram, Get thee out of thy country, and from thy kindred, and from thy father's house, unto a land that I will show thee: And I will make of thee a great nation, and I will bless thee, and make thy name great; and thou shalt be a blessing: And I will bless them that bless thee, and curse him that curseth thee: and in thee shall all families of the earth be blessed."

God promised Abraham and his family great blessings of wealth, royal ruling, and spiritual blessings. Spiritual blessings would include God's personal intervention into Abraham's family genealogy in selecting those that would carry the bloodline of the Messiah.

Jeremiah 23: 5-6 reads, "Behold, the days come, saith the Lord, that I will raise unto David a righteous Branch, and a King shall reign and prosper, and shall execute judgment and justice in the earth. In his days Judah shall be saved, and Israel shall dwell safely: and this is his name whereby he shall be called, The Lord Our Righteousness."

God's righteousness grew out as a branch from the throne of David as a fulfillment of the promise made to David by our Lord and Savior.

Joseph and Mary
Approximately (30BC–25AD)

THERE IS NOT A great deal of detailed information about Joseph and his family.

Matthew 1:18-21 reads, "Now the birth of Jesus Christ was on this wise: When as his mother Mary was espoused to Joseph, before they came together, she was found with child of the Holy Ghost. Then Joseph her husband, being a just man, and not willing to make her a public example, was minded to put her away privily. But while he thought on these things, behold, the angel of the Lord appeared unto him in a dream, saying, Joseph, thou son of David, fear not to take unto the Mary thy wife: for that which is conceived in her is of the Holy Ghost."

Joseph was the legal husband of Mary and the legal descendant of King David. Joseph was a just and God-fearing man that carried out God's commands and realized that God was directing him to take Mary as his wife and to raise her son.

Matthew 1:21 reads, "And she shall bring forth a son, and thus halt call his name Jesus: for he shall save his people from their sins."

Isaiah 7: 14 reads, "Therefore the Lord himself shall give you a sign; Behold a virgin shall conceive, and bear a son, and shall call his name Immanuel."

The prophecy provided by Isaiah was clear that a Savior would be born into this world. That prophecy was clearly fulfilled as Matthew described in the birth of Jesus of Nazareth.

Joseph was an ordinary man from a forgotten village who accepted and completed many extraordinary God-given tasks. Joseph did exactly what God asked of him and thereby was part of a miracle that would impact all of mankind. God chose Joseph because he was honorable, charitable, and proved his love for God with his obedience in keeping God's commandments.

Joseph and Mary were ordinary people who God entrusted to raise His only Son. God selected Joseph and Mary because of their love, humility, mercy, and willingness to be obedient to God's commandments and laws. They would follow God's laws and commandments throughout their lives in raising God's only son Jesus the Messiah. Joseph would continue working as a carpenter trying to provide for his growing family in the small city of Nazareth.

Jesus quickly grew in wisdom and strength under the direction of Joseph and Mary and with God's grace. Jesus grew up in a family where he gained an appreciation for hard work and understood the difficulties a poor family faced in providing for their daily needs.

Matthew details the royal bloodline of Joseph and how that passes on to Jesus (Son of David). Joseph and Mary have none of the character traits we see displayed in today's world. There was no mention of pride, power, wealth, or status. Joseph and Mary were unknown poor people who God selected because of their heart, soul and how they would follow God's direction in bringing into this world it's Savior, Messiah, Jesus the Christ.

APPLICATION

God's chosen people for His genealogy and royal bloodline were in some cases like Mary and Joseph. They were not kings or wealthy in the world's view, but they were kings and wealthy in God's view. God was able to see both the spirit of Mary and Joseph and their place in God's kingdom.

1 Corinthians 1:26-28 reads, "For ye see your calling, brethren, how that not many wise men after the flesh, not many mighty, and many noble, are called: But God hath chosen the foolish things of the world to confound the wise; and God hath chosen the weak things of the world to confound the things which are mightily; And base things of the world, and things which are despised, hath God chosen, yea, and things which are not, to bring to nought things that are:"

God does not value the things of the world. In fact, His values are in some cases almost the opposite of what the world views as important. Showing compassion for the poor, helping a neighbor in need, volunteering at a food bank, are as important as achieving great success and living the American dream.

Mary the mother of Jesus was highly favored by God not because of her great success or her status in the community, but because of her heart and willingness to obey. In fact, she was a complete unknown and had absolutely no status in society. She was young and had no possessions, no money, and was completely dependent on God's direction and love.

Luke 1:26-35 reads, "And in the sixth month the angel Gabriel was sent from God unto a city of Galilee, named Nazareth, To a virgin espoused to a man whose name was Joseph, of the house of David; and the virgin's name was Mary. And the angel came in unto her, and said, Hail, thou art highly favored, the Lord is with thee: blessed art thou among women. And when she saw him, she was troubled at his saying, and cast in her mind what manner of salutation this should be. And the angel said unto her, Fear not, Mary: for thou hast found favor with God. And, behold, thou shalt conceive in thy womb, and bring forth a son, and shalt call his name Jesus. He shall be great, and shall be called the Son of the Highest: and the Lord God shall give unto him the throne of his father David. And he shall reign over the house of Jacob for ever; and of his kingdom there shall be no end. Then said Mary unto the angel, How shall this be, seeing I know not a man? And the angel answered and said unto her, The Holy Ghost shall come upon thee, and the power of the Highest shall overshadow thee: therefore also that holy thing which shall be born of thee shall be called the Son of God."

A visit from an angel would be difficult for most people to handle. However, Mary with some assurances from the angel Gabriel was able to show great courage in understanding God's direction and in becoming obedient to God's plan. She put her complete trust in God and with all her love obeyed His will. Mary and the birth of Jesus were prophesied in Isaiah.

Isaiah 7:14 reads, "Therefore the Lord himself shall give you a sign; Behold, a virgin shall conceive, and bear a son, and shall call his name Immanuel."

We need to realize that God has a plan for us and we need to place our complete trust in him. We are not to rely on our own strength but on God's strength. God will come to us in times of weakness.

Joseph, Jesus' father was a direct descendant of King David. Joseph was a man of good standing in the community and made a living as a carpenter in Nazareth and the surrounding community. We know little about Joseph other than he followed Jewish law and it is believed he died a natural death prior to Jesus reaching the age of thirty.

As Mary, Joseph also had an encounter with an angel.

Matthew 1: 19-21 reads. "Then Joseph her husband, being a just man, and not willing to make her a public example, was minded to put her away privily. But while he thought on these things, behold, the angel of the Lord appeared unto him in a dream, saying, Joseph, thou son of David, fear not to take unto thee Mary thy wife: for that which is conceived in her is of the Holy Ghost. And she shall bring forth a son, and thou shalt call his name Jesus: for he shall save his people from their sins."

Joseph was a just man and showed great mercy in accepting Mary's condition and following God's direction. The angel assured Joseph that God was unfolding His plan with His son, Jesus. The new covenant was being fulfilled as God had promised in Jeremiah. God would place the new law on their hearts and minds. The Holy Spirit would come into the mind and heart of all believers.

Analysis

THERE IS ONLY ONE Bible and that Bible contains the Old Testament and the New Testament. Both the Old Testament and the New Testament apply equally to those that live under the new covenant of today.

2 Timothy 3:16 reads, "All scripture is given by inspiration of God, and is profitable for doctrine, for reproof, for correction, for instruction in righteousness."

The writers of the Bible were under the supernatural guidance of the Spirit of God. These scriptures were given by God to man to be used as a means to mature in the Christian faith, to test false doctrine, to correct and to instruct.

Proverbs 3:11 reads, "My son, despise not the chastening of the Lord; neither be weary of his correction: For whom the Lord loveth he correcteth; even as a father the son in whom he delighteth."

God loves and nurtures us as a father loves and nurtures his children. God in some cases will discipline those that who are trusting in their own skills and not trusting in God for his direction and blessings. In other cases, God will chasten and discipline in love those that need to purge their hearts of sin and self righteousness. Throughout history God has disciplined, chastened, and corrected his children in loving kindness to build faith and develop a closer relationship.

God unfolded his bloodline for His Son the Messiah beginning with Abraham (Approx. 2166-1953 BC). This genealogy for God's plan for Jesus Christ, the Son David, the Son of Abraham, encompassed over two thousand years and 42 generations. The Apostle Matthew's detailed genealogy clearly proves the Messiah was the King that was prophesied in the Old Testament. The Apostle Matthew's genealogy includes both men and women that represented a cross section for all of mankind.

ANALYSIS

The bloodline began with Abraham and a covenant that was made between God and Abraham. The covenant required Abraham not only to obey God's law but to live a life that was an example to the world as how to worship the one true God. God commanded Abraham to leave Mesopotamia and his father and move to Canaan. In turn, God promised Abraham that he would become the father of a great nation.

The covenant also revealed the depth of God's requirement for obedience for all of mankind. Abraham and his family would experience many blessings, but Abraham would also be asked to make the ultimate sacrifice of killing his beloved son, Isaac. Abraham followed God's command where most men would fail and God intervened with His grace and blessed Abraham for his obedience.

Abraham is considered the father of the great land of Israel and is the first in a long line of generations that leads to the Messiah. God tested Abraham and his obedience when He asked Abraham to sacrifice his son. Abrahams' obedience set in motion and introduces the final sacrifice, God's sacrifice of His son, Jesus Christ.

Our love for God and our willingness and desire to develop a closer relationship with God requires that we need to eliminate our love of self and the desires of the world. As Jesus said, "But many that are first shall be last; and the last shall be first." (Matt. 19:30)

Isaac was a gift from God to Abraham and Sarah and was used to carry God's royal bloodline forward. God, in this miracle reminds us that nothing is impossible for Him. He is the one and only true God that created the entire universe out of nothing. We need to pray continually, praising His name, thanking Him for His many blessings, and asking God for His grace and mercy in our daily lives. To experience the impossible in our daily lives we need to praise God with hearts open even in the worst of times. Isaac would carry the bloodline forward and be an important part of unfolding God's plan for all of mankind.

All of the patriarchs sinned, were disobedient and all experienced God's loving discipline. Jacob had a dream that confirmed that God's covenant with Abraham and Isaac was passed on to him. This dream also revealed that angels were moving between heaven and earth. Angels are mentioned many times throughout both the Old and New Testament as they serve and minister to God. They are able to take on many different forms, powers, and missions as they deliver God's blessings to God's people.

Jacob and the other patriarchs were contacted by angels with messages of blessings from God. They were continually under God's protection.

Genesis 22:11-12 reads, "And the angel of the Lord called unto him out of heaven, and said, Abraham, Abraham: and he said, Here am I. And he said, Lay not thine hand upon the Lad, neither do thou any thing unto him: for now I know that thou fearest God, seeing thou hast not withheld thy son, thine only son from me."

However, evil also exists on the earth and Satan and his fallen angels do have a limited amount of power that can have an impact on man's daily life. There are many avenues Satan can use to disrupt or break man's communion with God. Satan can appeal to man's pride, lust, or greed to cause man to sin by saying, doing, or thinking something that is harmful to his fellowman.

It is believed that Adam's sin caused God and the complete universe to cry out in great sorrow. The Garden of Eden was perfect in every way and provided for every need that Adam and Eve desired. This perfect paradise prepared by God for Adam and Eve would eventually dry up and turn into desert because of Satan's lie and the resulting sin. After Adam's sin Satan was allowed to unleash death and destruction upon all of mankind. Adam's decision to disobey God and sin would bring great pain for all of mankind. Man from that time forward would experience the sting of death, multiple types of all diseases, natural disasters, and many other unforeseen causes for pain and suffering.

However, God with great love would make the ultimate sacrifice that would allow man to escape this sentence of death and destruction. The Apostle Paul wrote creation would be freed from the bondage of decay.

Romans 8:21 reads, "Because the creature itself also shall be delivered from the bondage of corruption into the glorious liberty of the children of God."

God responded to man's sin be liberating mankind from the decay of the universe through His love and the gift of the His only Son.

The fall of man created a rip in the universe where death and destruction unfolded. Satan had lied to Eve and told her she would not die if she ate from the tree of the knowledge of good and evil. Satan is aware of man's weaknesses for greed and pride and will continue to create situations that will tempt man to become dissatisfied with God's blessings. Greed is a sin that causes man unnecessary pain and suffering and can be avoided if blessings are remembered and gratitude is considered a priority.

Jacob was the son of Isaac and Rebecca and the younger twin brother of Esau. Jacob had twelve sons and one daughter by his wives Leah, Rachel, and their handmaidens, Blhaha, and Zilpah. Jacob was in many respects a common man with many flaws and shortcomings. He was able to take advantage of his brother by purchasing Esau's birthright with a bowl of stew because Esau did not understand the importance of the birth right initially.

The eventual response from Esau was anger and his intent was to kill Jacob. It was the warning by Rebekah to Jacob that prevented evil from unfolding. We need to be aware of evil and take steps to avoid evil at all times. God was involved in Jacob's life and worked through Rebekah to prevent evil from prevailing. We live each day not knowing where evil is and depend on God to work through others to warn us of those who would do us harm. The importance of our prayer life cannot be understated since it is the one tool we have to communicate our concerns and thank God for his daily protection. We need to appreciate the fact that we are dealing with unknown powers and principalities and it is only by the grace of God and His angels that we are able to survive Satan and the attacks from his demons.

Judah was also selected to be in the Messiah's bloodline. He was a common man in many ways and was guilty of many sins. Judah was the fourth son of Jacob and Leah and brother to Reuben, Simeon, Lei, Issachar, and Zebulun. He also had one sister and six half brothers. Judah like his brothers hated Joseph and suggested selling Joseph as a slave to a caravan that was traveling to Egypt. Joseph was given special treatment from his father that caused a great deal of jealousy among the brothers. Jealousy and envy is like a cancer that can consume a man and can control his thinking and actions. Jealousy among sibling has been in existence since Cain and Abel.

We serve and worship a God who is divinely jealous of anything that separates man from God. Jealousy for man can be catastrophic and has the ability to take control of man's very being. It is one emotion that has the ability to change a person so dramatically that a person becomes lost in hate and envy.

Proverbs 14:30 reads, "A sound heart is the life of the flesh: but envy the rottenness of the bones."

Fallen man is subject to many emotions that are both beneficial and detrimental to his well-being. Unfortunately, Satan is aware of these frailties and will seduce man with promises of wealth and status to fill a need driven by pride, envy and jealousy.

Hebrews 13:5 reads, "Let your conversation be without covetousness; and be content with such things as ye have: for he hath said, I will never leave thee, nor forsake thee."

As believers we are locked for eternity into a relationship with our Lord and Savior. What we see and touch on this earth is only temporary and will all return to dust. Therefore, we need to be living a life that is focused on worshiping our God and Savior, following His will, and being obedient to His commands.

The Apostle Paul understood the meaning of contentment after being imprisoned, ship wreaked, stoned and left for dead. As God transformed his heart he learned to be content in whatever the situation. The Apostle Paul's first priority was to focus on learning God's will for his life and not to obsess on his own will. We come into this world with nothing and depart with nothing. Satan will tempt man with the promise of riches and many will fall into ruin and destruction trapped by their greed.

James 4:3 reads, "Ye ask, and receive not, because ye ask amiss, that ye may consume it upon your lust."

Requests made in prayer cannot be made with motives based on greed. Prayers need to be made with faith, without doubt and absent of excess, squander and waste. God does not give us what we want but what we need. Our prayers need to be focused first on God's kingdom and His righteousness and he will meet our needs.

Perez was God's choice to break through every barrier and carry the bloodline forward. It is God's purpose for us to move forward and break through barriers with our daily walk and ministries. We are often involved in long difficult battles with powers and principalities that require faith, patience, long suffering, and endurance to break barriers. God has promised to never leave us regardless of how hopeless the situation appears. God will allow us to break through difficult situations when it is within His purpose and His will for our lives. It is the blessing that was given to Perez that makes it possible for all barriers to be broken. No matter how hopeless a situation may appear we continue to pray in faith with the Holy Spirit's assistance. As we grow in faith the Holy Spirit takes on a greater role in our lives and directs our words, actions, ministers to our souls, and comforts our spirits.

ANALYSIS

1 Chronicles 27:3 reads, "Of the children of Perez was the chief of all the captains of the host for the first month."

The children of Perez held important positions within David's army of 288,000. Perez was given the great honor of carrying on the lineage of Judah and consequently, given the great honor of carrying on the lineage of the Messiah.

As believers we are all members of our divine heavenly Family. Our heavenly Father provides protection, cares for us in many ways, and meets our daily needs. God instructs us in many ways and will at times allow challenges to confront us so that we may gain an appreciation of what others are experiencing and react in a more effective and loving way.

The divine bloodline of the Messiah continued with Hezron the older of the two sons of Perez. Hezron was appointed by Moses and ordered by God to be the Prince over the tribe of Judah. As a tribal leader he worked with Moses in leading the Israelites out of Egypt and in to the wilderness. God blessed Hezron with the ability to lead and manage thousands of God's people under extremely challenging living conditions.

The gifts given to us by God are to be used in the service of others. It is by God's grace that we are given these gifts that work together to bless others in growing in faith. The gifts given by God to man are for the purpose of fulfilling His plan for each person's life. As in the case of Moses, God's plan included the gift of courage to Moses to allow the release of the Israelites from Egypt. Divine gifts from God to man are not always understood and do not always fit into the modern definition of gifts.

Ram also became a leader of the tribe of Judah like his father Hezron. The Apostle Paul outlined the qualities of a leader in the book of Timothy.

1 Timothy 3:1-7 reads, "This is a true saying, If a man desire the office of a bishop, he desireth a good work. A bishop then must be blameless, the husband of one wife, vigilant, sober, of good behavior, given to hospitality, apt to teach; Not given to wine, no striker, not greedy of filthy lucre; but patient, not a brawler, not covetous; One that ruleth well his own house, having his children in subjection with all gravity; For if a man know not how to rule his own house, how shall he take care of the church of God? Not a novice, lest being lifted up with pride he fall into the condemnation of the devil. Moreover he must have a good report of them which are without; lest he fall into reproach and the snare of the devil."

The bloodline for the Messiah included men like Ram who met the requirements for being a leader of the tribe and the Jewish people. It is believed that He was considered to be of good reputation, had self control, able to teach, not violent but gentle, and not a lover of money. Jesus lived his life on this earth as a servant not as a king. His example to us was to love one another with brotherly affection.

Amminadab like his father Ram and his grandfather Hezron was a leader of the tribe of Judah and the Israelites. Amminadab was also an ancestor of Boaz and David and therefore an ancestor of the Messiah. There are a number of examples of men that were blessed by God with management skills and given great responsibilities for caring for God's people. Joseph was sold into slavery by his brothers and later recognized by the Pharaoh of Egypt as a highly skilled manager for saving the people from starvation during seven years of famine. God placed Joseph in a place and time that was only known to Him to once again show how God's grace, mercy, and love is revealed for His people. Boaz was also a man of great insight and wisdom when he allowed the poor to gleam the fields of access grain during the harvest. This act of generosity was recognized by most as an act of sharing the wealth of a good harvest year. Wealthy land owners like Boaz realized the importance of building a good relationship with the community and those that worked long hours in the field year after year. The importance of generosity during a good harvest cannot be minimized during the poor and lean year of harvest when there is little access to be shared. An employee should be allowed to share in the success of a company when their efforts are responsible for the company's success.

Ruth 2:15-16 reads, "And when she was risen up to glean, Boaz commanded his young men, saying, Let her glean even among the sheaves, and reproach her not: And let fall also some of the handfuls of purpose for her, and leave them, that she may glean them, and rebuke her not."

Boaz took the gleaning of the fields to the next step to where he commanded his workers to intentionality leave grain in the field for Ruth and the poor. Boaz was a man of good reputation, generous and followed the law.

Nahshon the son of Amminadah was recorded as captain of the children of Judah.

Numbers 2:3 reads, "And on the east side toward the rising of the sun shall they of the standard of the camp of Judah pitch throughout their armies: and Nahshon the son of Ammindab shall be captain of the children of Judah."

Analysis

Sometime after the exile from Egypt God commanded Moses to take a census of all the men over 20 years of age in the twelve tribes. The encampment was composed and organized by the twelve tribes of Israel with three tribes located on all four sides surrounding the tabernacle. It is believed a total number of over 600,000 men were included in the census.

Nahshon was named captain of the tribe of Judah and was responsible for the daily operation of the tribe and meeting all the needs of the largest tribe of the twelve tribes. It is believed that the total number of men in the tribe of Judah over 20 years of age was over 75,000. It is estimated that this census count exceeded 200,000 when women and children were included. Nahshon had a great deal of management skills to meet the needs of many families that were in need of shelter, food, and security in a land where few resources were available.

God chose Nahshon for a very difficult and important job that had many difficult challenges.

Deuteronomy 1:15-18 reads, "So I took the chief of your tribes, wise men, and known, and made them heads over you, captains over thousands, and captains over hundreds, and captains over fifties, and captains over tens, and officers among your tribes. And I charged your judges at that time, saying, Hear the causes between your brethren, and judge righteously between every man and his brother, and the stranger that is with him. Ye shall not respect persons in judgment; but ye shall hear the small as well as the great; ye shall not be afraid of the face of man; for the judgment is God's: and the cause that is too hard for you, bring it unto me, and I will hear it. And I commanded you at that time all the things which ye should do."

Moses under God's direction decided who would be the chiefs of all the tribes. Nahshon was selected as captain of the tribe Judah, the largest tribe. It was Nahshon who commanded and located the army of Judah (est. 72,000 men) east of the tabernacle. It is believed that it was Nahshon who was part of the original group of Israelites who left Egypt and died wandering in the wilderness for forty years.

Obviously, managing thousands of people in the wilderness required a great deal of management and organizational skills. God gave Moses and his tribal captains great courage, wisdom and insight as to how to manage the tribes. The survival of the Israelites in the wilderness was only possible with God's wisdom and blessings that they received on a daily basis.

Salmon was the son of Nahshon, husband to Rahab, and Boaz was his son. It is believed that Salmon was part of the generation that entered the

Promised Land after the death of Moses. After Joshua became the leader of the Israelites he selected Salmon, a Prince of the tribe of Judah, to act as a spy to cross the Jordan River and enter into Jericho. Salmon was considered to be a man of courage and of good reputation among the people. Joshua selected Salmon and Phinehas as the two men to carry out a very dangerous mission to go behind enemy lines to determine troop strength and defenses.

Psalm 31:24 reads, "Be of good courage, and he shall strengthen your heart, all ye that hope in the Lord."

We all need to come to the point in our lives where we push self completely out of our lives in order experience true courage. We need to fall flat on our face in worship to our God and Creator and surrender all of our selfish ambitions and ask God for His will to be done in our lives. God the Creator of the entire universe is with us each day and in all situations.

Deuteronomy 31:8 reads, "And the Lord, he it is that doth go before thee; he will be with thee, he will not fail thee, neither forsake thee: fear not, neither be dismayed."

The bloodline of the Messiah included Salmon a young courageous man who was a prince in the tribe of Judah and who placed all of his trust in God as he crossed into the Promised Land.

Boaz the son of Salmon was also a Prince of the tribe of Judah. He was a wealthy land owner located near the city of Bethlehem. Boaz was a godly man who was kind, thoughtful, and sensitive to Ruth's station in life and her need for food and shelter. God would include Boaz and Ruth in the Messiah's bloodline as an example of God's love for all people regardless of their status in life and ethnicity. Our primary goal as a Christian is not to gain more wealth or a higher social status but to grow closer to God. When we grow closer to God he promises that we will lack no good thing. In other words, seeking to grow closer to God leads to desiring an even closer relationship with God. As Boaz, God shows his love to us in many ways as He prepares us to spend eternity with Him. The things of this world become less desirable as we grow in love with our Lord and Savior.

Ruth married Boaz and they had a son Obed. Obed (the son of Ruth a Moabite) represents an important link between the Gentile and the Messiah's bloodline. At this point, we see a clear connection between the bloodline of the Messiah and all nations and all of mankind. God's gift to all of mankind was Jesus the Christ, a gift that offers salvation to all those who believe. Obed was also the father of Jesse and the grandfather of David. He also represents a vital link between King David and fulfilling the prophecy of the Messiah (the Son of David).

God was deeply involved in the family of Jesse and ensured that the bloodline would continue with those that pleased Him. Jesse was a godly man and a farmer in Bethlehem of Judah. He raised sheep and goats with his eight sons. God became displeased with Saul the King of Judah because of his sins and asked Samuel His prophet to go select a new king from the family of Jesse. God asks the prophet Samuel to select and anoint David the youngest of the eight sons. God selects David the least qualified, youngest, and least experienced son who spent his days shepherding sheep. The prophet Samuel was obedient to God and anointed David to be King because David pleased God.

Isaiah prophesied that the Messiah would come from the family of Jesse. This prophecy occurred approximately 400 years before the anointing of David.

Isaiah 11:1-3 reads, "And there shall come forth a rod out of the stem of Jesse, and a Branch shall grow out of his roots. And the spirit of the Lord shall rest upon him, the spirit of wisdom and understanding, the spirit of counsel and might, the spirit of knowledge and of the fear of the Lord; And shall make him of quick understanding in his fear of the Lord: and he shall not judge after the sight of his eyes, neither reprove after the hearing of his ears:"

The bloodline of the Messiah travels through the family of Jesse to King David. God's hand was directly on these selections for the heirs of the Messiah's bloodline. David was not selected because of his experience and station in life, but because of what God saw in him and what he could become. Obedience to God's word is the key to pleasing God and allowing blessings to flow, open doors, and experience God's grace.

Like Moses, David was selected by God to be transformed from a shepherd into one of the world's greatest leaders. King David was able to resolve many of the tribal conflicts in the area and to consolidate Judah and Israel. King David under God's direction took a war-torn area and transformed it into a wealthy trading center by bringing the tabernacle to Jerusalem, creating a capital for the area, and expanding the kingdom from Egypt to the Euphrates valley.

Courage was a common attribute that was displayed by both Moses and David after being anointed by God. David first displayed his courage when he took a sling and killed the nine foot giant Goliath. This act of bravery got the attention of King Saul and David was installed as commander of the army. David's courage served him well as he encountered many battles and conflicts throughout his 40 year reign as King. One of those conflicts actually involved King Saul when he tried to kill David a number of times out of jealously. Courage is an attribute that everyone wants due to the fact that it demands respect and is considered to be of good character. Bravery or valor is a quality of spirit that enables a person to face danger and difficulties with some degree of confidence and determination.

David was also blessed by God as a talented musician and poet. King Saul enjoyed David's musical ability and invited him to play for him and his court. God used David's ability as a poet to write major portions of The Book of Psalms. God obviously through His infinite wisdom and time blesses people with talents that are to be used to future His glory.

However, David was also a man of frailties that eventually caused him to fall out of favor with God at the end of his reign. These sins prevented him from building the Temple that he had planned for years to build for God.

1 Chronicles 28:2-6 reads, "Then David the king stood up upon his feet, and said, Hear me, my brethren, and my people: As for me, I had in mine heart to build a house of rest for the ark of the covenant of the Lord, and for the footstool of our God, and had made ready for the building: But God said unto me, Thou shalt not build a house for my name, because thou hast been a man of war, and hast shed blood. Howbeit the Lord God of Israel chose me before all the house of my father to be king over Israel for ever: for he hath chosen Judah to be ruler, and of the house of Judah, the house of my father; and among the sons of my father he liked me to make me king over all Israel: And of all my sons, (for the Lord hath given me many sons,) he hath chosen Solomon my son to sit upon the throne of the kingdom of the Lord over Israel. And he said unto me, Solomon thy son, he shall build my house and my courts: for I have chosen him to be my son, and I will his father."

The actual transition of power and the bloodline lineage to Solomon was not without great difficulty. The transition was marked with tragedy as one older brother of Solomon killed another brother for fear of not being appointed heir to the throne. King David at the end conceded that God had chosen Solomon to build the Temple. David's charge to Solomon was to serve God with a perfect heart and a willing mind.

ANALYSIS

1 Chronicles 28:9 reads, "And thou, Solomon my son, know thou the God of thy father, and serve him with perfect heart and with a willing mind: for the Lord searcheth all hearts, and understandeth all imaginations of the thoughts: if thou seek him, he will be found of thee; but if thou forsake him, he will cast thee off for ever."

God blessed Solomon with great wisdom and understanding and because of those blessings he was able to accumulate great power and wealth. However, Solomon could not control his thoughts of foreign women and their worship of foreign gods. As these foreign women clung to him in his old age he could no longer keep God's commandments. The lesson is clear that great wealth and power will not please God without a pure heart and a mind that is free of immoral thoughts.

God's penalty for worshiping other gods is severe and can impact many generations. In the case of Solomon, his sins resulted in the kingdom of Israel being spilt and the people revolting.

1 Kings 11:11 reads, "Wherefore the Lord said unto Solomon, Forasmuch as this is done of thee, and thou hast not kept my covenant and my statutes, which I have commanded thee, I will surely rend the kingdom from thee, and will give it to thy servant"

Solomon's sin had a direct impact on his kingdom, his son Rehoboam, and the people of Israel. Solomon placed a heavy tax on the people of Israel and placed many in forced labor to build the Temple and many other structures.

King Rehoboam lacked the wisdom of his father and made a number of bad decisions that lead to the land of Israel being split into two kingdoms. The northern kingdom contained ten tribes that revolted due to the high taxes and forced labor situation. Only the tribes of Judah and Benjamin remained with King Rehoboam in Jerusalem.

Today, the worship of wooden and stone images of gods has been replaced with the worship of money, possessions and pride.

Exodus 20:5-6 reads, "Thou shalt not bow down thyself to them, nor sever them: for I the Lord God am a jealous God, visiting the iniquity of the fathers upon the children unto the third and fourth generation of them that hate me; And showing mercy unto thousands of them that love me, and keep my commandments."

Sin is a massive problem for man and can be the cause of severe pain and suffering for many generations. Breaking the chains of sin and its dire consequences on all of mankind was made possible with the bloodline of the Messiah and the ultimate sacrifice of God's only son, Jesus Christ.

King Abijah like his father Rehoboam did not have a close relationship with God. However, because of God' close relationship with David, God did provide a lamp to Abijah that would provide some light and allow Abijah to have a son Asa. In this situation, God showed his grace and mercy to King Abijah because of His covenant with David.

1 Samuel 13:14 reads, "But now thy kingdom shall not continue: the Lord hath sought him a man after his own heart, and the Lord hath commanded him to be captain over his people, because thou hast not kept that which the Lord commanded thee."

God appointed David as the divine King of Israel (a man after his own heart). David was a man of great faith and loved his Lord and Savior greatly. However, King David was far from perfect and had many problems with sin.

Asa became king over Judah for forty one years because he followed in the steps of David and was obedient to God's commands. King Asa did right in the sight of the Lord as did David, removed all the idols, and expelled all those that were perverted. He was able to fortify the cities and ruled over a long period of peace. Asa's reign ended when he no longer relied on God for direction and entered into agreements with the king of Syria. Asa's rule ended badly as he mistreated the people, contacted disease and lost his faith in God.

Faith and trust in our Lord and Savior is developed and strengthen by reading and studying God's word.

Romans 10:17 reads, "So then faith cometh by hearing, and hearing by the word of God."

Jeremiah 29:12-13 reads, "Then shall ye call upon me, and ye shall go and pray unto me, and I will hearken unto you. And ye shall seek me, and find me, when ye shall search for me with all your heart."

Jehoshaphat the son of Asa reigned as the King of Judah for twenty five years in the bloodline for the Messiah. The people of Judah were blessed by Jehoshaphat's rule and his willingness to send out the Levites and priests to instruct the people of God's law. As Asa, King Jehoshaphat condemned the worship of idols and exiled the perverted. Jehoshaphat was obedient to God's word, commandments and walked in faith. Walking in faith requires a strong determination to follow God's plan for our life and to study His word for daily instruction. Life is not easy and is full of disappointments, challenges, and requires God's strength each day.

James 1:1-6 reads, "James, a servant of God and of the Lord Jesus Christ, to the twelve tribes which are scattered abroad, greeting. My brethren, count it all joy when ye fall into divers temptations; Knowing this, that the trying of your faith worketh patience. But let patience have her perfect work, that ye may be perfect and entire, wanting nothing. If any of you lack wisdom, let him ask of God, that giveth to all men liberally, and upbraideth not; and it shall be given him. But let him ask in faith, nothing waving. For he that wavereth is like a wave of the sea driven with the wind and tossed."

God is looking for those with a pure heart, those who have chosen to be obedient, and those who have given their all. God is looking to mold each man's life with challenges that will test his faith and purify his purpose and plan. God has promised to be with each man with each step as He unfolds his amazing plan.

It is believed that King Jehoram, Jehoshaphat's son began his short reign of 8 years at the age of thirty two. Jehoram married Athaliah the daughter of Jezebel and fell under the influences of pagan worship and other perversions. King Jehoram quickly killed a number of his brothers, reversed many of his father's efforts to eliminate idols, created great religious turmoil, and increased the conflict with many of the neighboring tribes. It is believed that Elijah the prophet cursed the rule of Jehoram that resulted in a plague upon the land and its people. Jehoram's rule ended with his body being buried in an unmarked grave outside the city of Jerusalem.

The pride of life, the lust of the eyes, and the lust of the flesh has always been a major problem for all of mankind. God has commanded man not to love the things of the world. The world will pass away along with all things. God is eternal and has always been and will always be.

Those that love the world and have invested all of their lives in building wealth will use any means possible to protect that wealth. Spending time and money in any effort to save souls and spread the gospel message has always been considered ridiculous and counterproductive by these individuals. In other words, the love of God and the obedience to His commandments has no place in a world of greed, pride, and lust.

1 John 2:15-17 reads, "Love not the world, neither the things that are in the world. If any man love the world, the love of the Father is not in him. For all that is in the world, the lust of the flesh, and the lust of the eyes, and the pride of life, is not of the Father, but is of the world. And the world

passeth away, and the lust thereof: but he that doeth the will of God abideth for ever."

The next person listed in the Messiah bloodline was King Uzziah. King Uzziah reigned for 52 years as King of Judah and was considered be a good king that pleased God. Unfortunately, after experiencing many great achievements, pride became a major problem for King Uzziah when he performed duties that were reserved for only Priests. He entered the sanctuary of the Lord's Temple and burned incense on the altar. When he was confronted by the priests for his sinful actions he became angry. The Lord responded by inflicting King Uzziah with leprosy. King Uzziah spent the remainder of his reign in isolation.

Proverbs 16:18 reads, "Pride goeth before destruction, and a haughty spirit before a fall."

Pride acts as a barrier that will block a person from experiencing God's greatest blessings. Pride will prevent a person from walking through God's plan for their life and it will prevent a person from accepting and applying valuable council. Man needs to remember who he is.

Pride has always been a problem for all of mankind and began with Satan. Pride is a sin of man that will result at some time in experiencing God's judgment. Pride is the arrogant, inflated opinion of self that causes an attitude of superiority over others. God's commands us to love our neighbor and in no way to feel superior to our neighbor.

Ephesians 2:4-6 reads, "But God, who is rich in mercy, for his great love wherewith he loved us, Even when we were dead in sins, hath quickened us together with Christ, by grace ye are saved; And hath raised us up together, and made us sit together in heavenly places in Christ Jesus:"

Our salvation is a gift from God and is no way related to man's efforts or any work completed by man. God's grace and His blessings are a reflection of His love for us and in no way associated with man's pride or his sin.

Jotham continued the bloodline of the Messiah, was the son of King Uzziah, and reigned as King in Judah for sixteen years. He was considered to be a godly king, but failed to eliminate the worship of idols in Judah.

Sin has always been a problem for man and the worship of idols is one sin that continues to persist today. Idols are created by the world and can take on many forms and are used to replace the worship of God. Even though the world promotes the worship of money, pleasure and status, we often hear that many are disillusioned and still feel unfulfilled when they achieve the world's goals of wealth, pleasure and status. We are created in

Analysis

God's image and naturally require a close relationship with the Holy Spirit as we live out our daily lives following His direction and His will for our lives.

Ecclesiastes 3:11 reads, "He hath made every thing beautiful in his time: also he hath set the world in their heart, so that no man can find out the work that God maketh from the beginning to the end."

Man's heart desires eternity with his Creator and cannot be satisfied with the temporary life he lives on this earth. Man knows God has made everything beautiful in its time and desires to know God's will and purpose for his life. None of the world's idols are going to fill that void.

Ahaz the son of Jotham was generally known as one of the evil kings of Judah. He made a number of bad alliances that put Judah in danger and returned to the worship of idols.

Romans 8:28 reads, "And we know that all things work together for good to them that love God, to them who are the called according to his purpose."

God is the Sovereign Creator of all things and is in control of all things including both evil and good. God created man with free will and has allowed him to accept or reject God's love and commands. God can use the evil of this world for His purpose to bring about glory for those who love Him and keep HIs commandments. For example, God hardened the heart of the Pharaoh as a way to release the Israelites, he used Babylon to capture and discipline the Israelites for their worship of idols, and He used Rome and Pilate to send Jesus to his death and bring salvation to all of mankind.

Hezekiah the son of Ahaz reigned for twenty nine years and was a great and godly king. He eliminated idolatry from the kingdom and a great reformation took place during his reign. Hezekiah placed his trust in God and prayed to God for protection when the Assyrian army attacked Jerusalem. God sent out an angel who struck down one hundred and eighty five thousand Assyrian soldiers. Hezekiah ended his days in peace and prosperity and was buried with the sepulchres of the sons of David.

God heard Hezekiah's prayer for help and responded by sending an angel to destroy his enemy. God requires that we ask for our needs and desires in payer.

Matthew 7:7 reads,"Ask, and it shall be given you, seek, and ye shall find; knock, and it shall be opened unto you:"

Prayer is an extremely important part of the Christian's life. Prayer is the method for how each Christian communicates with God on a daily basis. Our prayers should follow the prayer that Jesus gave the disciples. This prayer praised God, thanked him for His many blessings, asked for the forgiveness of our many sins, and asked that our needs and the needs of others may be met. All of this prayer was submitted in the name of the Lord Jesus Christ.

We worship an all powerful all knowing God who is able to remove any obstacle, change any outcome, and love all sinners. God hears each and every prayer and answers each prayer in His time and way. God sees all and hears all and is able to see the past and the future for all of His creation. God's answer to our prayers may involve many different people, different situations, different times, and our personal maturity and motives. In other words, God's answer to our prayers may be obvious or maybe impossible for us to fully appreciate. In some situations we may never understand God's answer. The fastest way to gain an appreciation and scope of how God has answered our prayers is to review the past and count all of God's blessings.

Manasseh was included in the bloodline of the Messiah as the son of Hezekiah. At the age of twelve he became co-ruler of Judah for eleven years and for forty four years as sole ruler of Judah. He was also known as one of the wickedest kings to rule Judah. He was taken to Babylon as a prisoner where he repented of his evil ways and was restored as King.

Jeremiah 17:9 reads, "The heart is deceitful above all things, and desperately wicked: who can know it?

All men were born into sin and under the penalty of death because of the decisions made by Adam and Eve. All Christians claim to love God, but all fail to keep His commandments even on a daily basis. God is sovereign and is in control of all evil and good things. God allowed the persecution of the early church and guided it as it moved from Jerusalem to many different locations throughout the world. Discipline is used by God in response to sin and this discipline may come from many different sources.

Amon ruled for only two years. He was the son of Manasseh, but did not learn from his father's mistakes and continued with the evil worship of idols. King Amon was included in the Messiah bloodline and represented the sin of mankind and the evil that permeates men's soul.

Josiah was the son of Amon and began his rule of thirty-one years at the age of eight. King Josiah was a child that had the heart for the Lord and His commandments.

Proverbs 22:6 reads, "Train up a child in the way he should go: and when he is old, he will not depart from it."

Children are a precious gift from God that requires our instruction as to how to live a Christ-centered life. Jesus instructed his disciples that they needed to become like children in order to enter the kingdom of God. As a child is completely dependent on a parent, a man needs to become completely dependent on God.

No decision should be made without first requesting God's help and His will. The point is that God is always recognized first in all decisions and has our complete devotion.

Philippians 4:6 reads, "Be careful for noting; but in every thing by prayer and supplication with thanksgiving let your requests be made known unto God."

Jechoniah was the son of Josiah. King Jechoniah was king for only a few months before he was captured by the Babylon army and King Nebuchadnezzar. King Jechoniah and those that were related to him and reported to him were all relocated and imprisoned in Babylon for many years while Nebuchadnezzar was in power. King Jechoniah did that which was evil in the sight of the Lord.

Certainly one of God's greatest creations is man and his ability to use free will to make decisions to accept or reject God's many blessings. Man was also created in God's image with the ability to commune with God with his soul and spirit. Man is a creative masterpiece that was given countless abilities and talents.

Free will allows man the freedom to reject evil and express his love for God and obey God's commandments. Pride, self love, and the worship of idols has always been a problem for man. Satan continues to use these weaknesses to drive men to an early grave without any regard for their own soul.

Salathiel was the son of Jechoniah and was held captive in Babylon alone with the rest of the royal family. There is little known about King Salathiel and his activities during this time period. In this case, God's reaction to the idol worship at this point in time was the captivity of this King and his royal family.

Exodus 20:5 reads, "Thou shalt not bow down thyself to them, nor serve them: for I the Lord thy God am a jealous God, visiting the iniquity of the fathers upon the children unto the third and fourth generation of them that hate me;"

Obviously, God hates idolatry and the descendants of those involved in idol worship will inherit the consequences in the form of disease and other misfortunes. Idolatry is extremely dangerous due to the fact it provokes God's wrath. Unfortunately, today man has fallen to the point where idolatry is a common practice and is not recognized as a sin. Today, men are consumed by worshiping self, pleasure, and possessions rather than worshiping God. This idol worship will provoke God's wrath and many will suffer the consequences.

Zerubbabel the son of Salathiel was also in the Messiah's bloodline and was allowed to return to Jerusalem from Babylon. God worked through Zerubbabel as He provided the direction and leadership that made the rebuilding of the temple possible.

Obedience to God's commandments is the first step that needs to be taken before more of God's will is unfolded for our lives. Obedience can be difficult for some Christians because of the pressures inflicted by the world and weakness of the fallen man to always think in terms of self and how the ego is impacted. Many opportunities to be involved in God's plans are missed or delayed because of egos being offended due to lack of recognition.

Christians should complete each task with their best effort and thank God for each opportunity. However, taking credit for any success without thanking God would be sin.

Colossians 3:17 reads, "And whatsoever ye do in word or deed, do all in the name of the Lord Jesus, giving thanks to God and the Father by him."

As Christians we do all things in the presences of a sovereign God and need to be in the spirit of thanksgiving and humility as we live out the life given to us by God the Father.

1 Peter 5:5 reads, "Likewise, ye younger, submit yourselves unto the elder. Yea, all of you be subject one to another, and be clothed with humility: for God resisteth the proud, and giveth grace to the humble."

Abiud was the son of Zerubbabel and part of the Messiah's bloodline. We know little about the Abiud listed in the Gospel of Mathew. However, God created His church from millions of unknown people over thousands of years that worshiped the one true God. These millions of unknown believers experienced persecution in many different forms. As Christians we need to enter our churches in complete humility with a profound appreciation of all the millions of unknown believers who in many cases freely gave their lives so that we may worship in God's house.

Eliakim was the next in line as part of the Messiah's bloodline as the son of Adiud. Isaiah the prophet was able to prophesy the arrival of God's perfect gift to all of mankind and that gift was Jesus Christ the Messiah.

God Almighty through His infinite wisdom was able to provide mankind a path to salvation.

Azor was the son of Eliakim and was another person we know little about that was part of the Messiah bloodline. We pray each day that God's will would be made complete in our daily lives and that we would experience His grace and love throughout each day. There are millions of unknown people living and working each day that are in God's will and are experiencing God's blessings. Genesis 3:19 reads, "In the sweat of thy face shalt thou eat bread, till thou return unto the ground; for out of it wast thou taken: for dust thou art, and unto dust shalt thou return." Man is condemned to work to provide for themselves and their families. However, the life of a Christian takes on a new meaning and dimension that includes having a personal relationship with their Savior and Lord, knowing that God has a specific plan for their lives, and that their lives will continue in heaven.

Sadoc was the son of Azor. The name Sadoc was believed to mean a righteous man that was honest, just, and lawful. Jesus was the only man to live a sin free righteous life. Consequently, it is impossible for man to live a sin free life and achieve righteousness through obedience. We are all guilty of sin and are completely dependent on God's grace and the gift of His Son.

Isaiah 61:10 reads, "I will greatly rejoice in the Lord, my soul shall be joyful in my God; for he hath clothed me with the garments of salvation, he hath covered me with the robe of righteousness, as a bridegroom decketh himself with ornaments, and as a bride adorneth herself with her jewels."

Jeremiah 23:5-6 reads, "Behold, the days come, saith the Lord, that I will raise unto David a righteous Branch, and a King shall reign and prosper, and shall execute judgment and justice in the earth."

The bloodline of the Messiah made it possible for our Savior to be born and to live a sin free life. It was God's grace that may it possible for believers to be covered by a robe of righteousness and to be welcomed to spend eternity with our Savior and Lord.

Achim means that the Lord will establish. He was the son of Sadoc and part of the Messiah's bloodline. As Christians we are to be fully engaged in presenting the Gospel to all that will hear. This is our reasonable service as a follower and servant of Jesus Christ.

1 Peter 5:10 reads, "But the God of all grace, who hath called us unto his eternal glory by Christ Jesus, after that ye have suffered a while, make you perfect, stablish, strengthen, settle you."

We are established with Christ and anointed by God for the purpose of strengthening our hearts in all good works.

Eliud was the son of Achim which is believed to mean, God is my praise. We praise God throughout each day as we recognize His many blessings. We praise Him for His indescribable power, for His knowledge of all things present, past and future, and for His immeasurable love for us. God is the Alpha and Omega, the beginning and the end, King of Kings and Lord of Lords.

2 Chronicles 5:13-14 reads, "It came even to pass, as the trumpeters and singers were as one, to make one sound to be heard in praising and thanking the Lord; and when they lifted up their voice with the trumpets and cymbals and instruments of music, and praised the Lord, saying, For he is good; for his mercy endureth for ever: that then the house was filled with a cloud, even the house of the Lord; So that the priests could not stand to minister by reason of the cloud: for the glory of the Lord had filled the house of God."

One day we will all be filled with God's Spirit as one as we worship and praise our Lord and Savior for His mighty works and His endless grace and love.

Eleazar the son of Eliud was also included in the Messiah's bloodline. There are a number of men named Eleazar in the Bible. There are millions of unknown Christians that have been involved in building and growing the church. Many Christians have died for their faith over the centuries. Their memorial is the existence of the church which has lasted for over two thousand years.

A servant of God is a person who is always available to God's will.

Isaiah 6:8 reads, "Also I heard the voice of the Lord, saying, Whom shall I send, and who will go for us? Then said I, Here am I; send me."

A servant follows God and is satisfied with his blessings.

Luke 9:23 reads, "And he said to them all, If any man will come after me, let him deny himself, and take up his cross daily, and follow me."

Matthan was the son of Eleazar. The word Matthan means a gift from God. The birth of a child is normally considered a precious gift from God and a great responsibility for both the mother and father. God has given each of us the precious gift of life and the opportunity to create and live on this amazing planet earth. God's greatest gift was the gift of His Son and the grace that allows each person to experience His love and the forgiveness of sin.

Jacob was the son of Matthan according to Matthew. The name Jacob is recorded a number of times throughout the Bible and in this case Matthew records Jacob as the father of Joseph the husband of Mary.

The genealogy of a family was extremely important at that time for the purpose of showing the rank, power and social status of a family in the community. The genealogy recorded by the Apostle Matthew of Jesus Christ the Messiah is extremely important for a number of reasons. First, it clearly documents how the prophecies of the Old Testament were unfolded in the New Testament.

Jeremiah 23:5-6 reads, "Behold, the days come, saith the Lord, that I will raise unto David a righteous Branch, and a king shall reign and prosper, and shall execute judgment and justice in the earth."

Out of King David's family tree the Messiah was born who will someday execute judgment and justice over all of mankind.

Joseph the son of Jacob was married and became husband to Mary the mother of Jesus.

Matthew 1: 20-21 reads, "But while he thought on these things, behold, the angel of the Lord appeared unto him in a dream, saying, Joseph, thou son of David, fear not to take unto thee Mary thy wife: for that which is conceived in her is of the Holy Ghost. And she shall bring forth a son, and thou shalt call his name Jesus: for he shall save his people from their sins."

Joseph was considered to be a just man and an obedient man to God's direction. Joseph followed the directions given by God's angel and would continue to depend on God's directions and protection in a time of great danger. Sin is an evil that that can be chosen by man that will infect and destroy his heart and soul. Sin is extremely dangerous and can bring about great suffering that can be passed down for generations.

God allowed Joseph and Mary to give birth to His Son, Jesus, a child that would bring salvation to millions of people that were lost in their sin. The decision to believe in Jesus and follow His commandments is the only requirement needed to receive God's blessings for eternity.

Conclusion

God created a number of covenants that acted as the foundation and framework for God's bloodline and His plan for the salvation for all of mankind. The first covenant made by God, required Noah to build a massive boat that would provide for a new start for mankind and great blessings from God to Noah and his family.

Genesis 6:13-14 reads, "And God said unto Noah, The end of all flesh is come before me; for the earth is filled with violence through them; and, behold, I will destroy them with the earth. Make thee an ark of gopher wood; rooms shalt thou make in the ark, and pitch it within and without with pitch."

The second covenant was made with Abraham that required Abraham and his family to move from Mesopotamia to Canaan, where Abraham's family would be blessed and grow in great numbers.

Genesis 12:1-2 reads, "Now the Lord had said unto Abram, Get thee out of thy country, and from thy kindred, and from thy father's house, unto a land that I will show thee: And I will make thee a great nation, and I will bless thee, and make thy name great; and thou shalt be a blessing."

The third covenant by God was revealed by Nathan the prophet to King David. David was loved greatly by God for his heart and for his great love for His Creator. King David was courageous, he was obedient to the Lord, he was repentant of his many sins, and he worked hard to plan for the building of the Lord's house.

1 Chronicles 17:11-15 reads, "And it shall come to pass, when thy days be expired that thou must go to be with thy fathers, that I will raise up thy seed after thee, which shall be of thy sons; and I will establish his kingdom. He shall build me a house, and I will stablish his throne forever. I will be his father, and he shall be my son: and I will not take my mercy away from him, as I took it from him that was before thee: But I will settle him in mine

Conclusion

house and in my kingdom for ever: and his throne shall be establish for evermore. According to all these words, and according to all this vision, so did Nathan speak unto David."

David loved God's perfect word and spent many days writing and meditating on God's word. It is believed that David was the author of over 70 psalms. Psalm 119: 47-48 reads, "And I will delight myself in thy commandments, which I have loved. My hands also will I lift up unto the commandments, which I have loved; and I will meditate in thy statutes." God did bless David with wisdom and understanding as he spent his days meditating on God's word. God blessed David by allowing David to be included in the bloodline of the Messiah (The Son of David).

The last covenant or the Mosaic Covenant was with the people of Israel. The covenant between God and his people is a promise that they would become a great nation if they obeyed His word.

Exodus 19:3-6 reads, "And Moses went up unto God, and the Lord called unto him out of the mountain, saying, Thus shalt thou say to the house of Jacob, and tell the children of Israel; Ye have seen what I did unto the Egyptians, and how I bare you on eagles' wings, and brought you unto myself. Now therefore, if ye will obey my voice indeed, and keep my covenant, then ye shall be a peculiar treasure unto me above all people: for all the earth is mine: And ye shall be unto me a kingdom of priests, and a holy nation. These are the words which thou shalt speak unto the children of Israel."

God has kept His promise and the covenant that He would make the land of Israel a great nation and its people a treasure unto God. This covenant of protection by God allowed the bloodline of the Messiah to come to fulfillment and allowed God's plan for man's salvation to be available to all mankind.

The Gospel of Matthew begins the generations of Jesus Christ (the Messiah) with Abraham. God created a covenant with Abraham, his son Isaac, Isaac's son Jacob, and Jacob's twelve sons. The twelve sons of Jacob would be the fathers of the twelve tribes of Israel and the chosen nation of God. God blessed Abraham and the Israelites that established the nation of Israel. They were the people (the Israelites) that finally occupied the Promised Land. This chosen nation of God would serve as a leader to all other nations in following God's word and living as an example of an obedient people. Israel's message was the promise of a Savior and Messiah that would come for the salvation of mankind. Unfortunately, as prophesied many did deny Christ and still today refuse to recognize Jesus as the Messiah and Savior for all of mankind. 1 Peter 2:9 reads, "But ye are a chosen generation, a royal priesthood, a holy nation, a peculiar people; that ye should show forth the praises of him who hath called you out of darkness into his marvelous light."

The Apostle Matthew recorded the fourteen generations that exist between Abraham and King David. Included in this listing of ancestors of the Messiah are the patriarchs. Abraham is known as the "father of a multitude" due to the fact he had a close relationship with God and was blessed by God to be the father of a great nation of people. Isaac, Abraham's son, was a man of great faith due to the fact he knew God and trusted Him with his life. Isaac never forgot that God saved him from death and provided a ram for the sacrifice. He grew up as a miracle baby from a father who was over one hundred years old and a mother over ninety years old. Isaac was also blessed by the fact that he was taught by a father of great faith, a man that lived before the law and the commandments delivered by Moses. Isaac married only one wife, Rebekah, who he loved with great passion throughout his entire life. Jacob was the son of Isaac and the father and patriarch for the twelve tribes of Judah. It was Jacob's twelve sons that would eventually grow into the twelve tribes that would move into the Promised Land and establish the nation of Israel. Judah was held in high esteem as the fourth son of Jacob and Leah. Judah took on a leadership role of the Jacob family and negotiated a smooth transition into the land of Goshen (eastern part of delta of the Nile). Jacob predicted that the tribe of Judah would grow to have superior power over the other tribes and grow in prosperity. It was the tribe of Judah after the enslavement in Egypt that acted as a united effort to bring the Hebrew people together. The tribe of Judah preserved the true religion, maintained and preserved the priesthood, and ensured the ceremonies of the temple. However, Judah was involved in selling his brother Joseph and some other sinful acts during his early life. Perez was the next in the line of the genealogy of the Messiah and was blessed greatly with the honor of carrying on the lineage of Judah. This blessing was remembered by the Jewish people as a blessing that was beyond measure. Hezron was chosen by God to be the leader of the tribe of Judah just as his father Perez and his grandfather Judah were chosen by God to be leaders. God's plan included these men as well as many others to unfold God's plan and the bloodline for the Messiah. These men were chosen by God and not self-appointed or planned to be leaders. It is also believed that Ram was alive during the time

CONCLUSION

of Moses and the exodus from Egypt. He would have been another leader of the tribe of Judah and a confidant of Moses and Aaron. Amminadab meaning (a people of liberty) was again believed to be a man of leadership within the tribe of Judah and in the lineage of the Messiah. It is believed he was born in Egypt and probably died in the wilderness as a leader of the tribe of Judah. It is believed that Nahshon was the leader of the tribe of Judah when the Jewish people were traveling through the Sinai. It is believed that Amminadab would not have entered into the Promised Land, but his son, Nahshon and his grandson Salmon, may have received the blessing to enter the Promised Land. Salmon was the great, great, grandfather of King David and was from the tribe of Judah. He was also living during the time of Joshua and would have been involved in the capturing of the land of Canaan the Promised Land. Boaz was a wealthy land owner in Bethlehem in Judea and the son of Salmon and Rahab. He was also in the genealogy of the Messiah, Christ Jesus. Ruth immigrated to Bethlehem with her mother-in-law Naomi. Ruth married Boaz and they had a son Obed. Obed was the father of Jesse and the grandfather of David which included in the lineage of the Messiah, Jesus Christ. A new life would come out of the family of Jesse and out of the tribe Judah. This new life was coming from the family of Jesse and his son David through which the Messiah would be born. The Spirit of the Lord came upon David when he was anointed King and would rest upon David's descendants. The Holy Spirit would bring upon David and his descendants (the Messiah, Jesus Christ) the knowledge and the fear of the Lord, the spirit of understanding and council, and the ability to rule justly. It was the grace of God that selected David to be chosen. David realized and understood this relationship was due to God's grace and nothing he could achieve. He loved God with all his heart and soul and strived to be obedient in all ways.

The first listing of kings and leaders recorded by Matthew included great men of God that had close relationships with their Creator. They were faithful men, but not perfect in any way.

The second listing of the ancestors of the Messiah by Matthew began after King David and ended before the exile of the Israelites to Babylon. Solomon was the son of David and a man of great wisdom. It is also believed that Solomon wrote the book of Proverbs as a way to share his wisdom in honoring and following God's commands. He also wrote the book Song of Solomon to show the joy of love from God. It is believed that it was God that convinced David to appoint Solomon as king. Solomon as a fallen man had many faults that lead him to sin against God in many ways. These sins did not go unnoticed and eventually Solomon did pay for these sins with the loss of his rule as King. Solomon's son Rehoboam did not listen or seek God's wisdom but listen to the council of those that were in his court. The result was disastrous. Rehoboam lost control of the northern kingdom, Israel and remained the King for only the southern kingdom of Judah. God's displeasure with Solomon and Rehoboam caused the kingdoms to collapse without God's blessings and protection. Rehoboam ruled Judah for seventeen years and during that time he made many idols for the people to worship the Moabite and Ammonite gods. God demands that we worship only Him and that He will not tolerate the worship of any other gods. God is the same today as He was when He created all of the universe. Abijah made many of the same mistakes as his father Rehoboam and was never able to consolidate the north and south kingdoms. King Abijah like his father Rehoboam did not have a close relationship with God and was deeply involved in the worship of pagan gods. King Asa, Abijah's son assembled the people to worship the one true God and made a promise to follow and obey the laws of the Jewish people. King Asa made a great sacrifice of the animals that had been taken as the spoil of wars. God rewarded Asa and the Jewish people with peace for a period of time. Jehosphaphat the son of Asa ruled over Judah for 25 years and was the fourth King of Judah. King Jehoshaphat's son Jehoram was the oldest of seven sons and would succeed him as King. It is generally agreed that Judah did experience a great many blessings, prosperity, and peace because of Jehoshaphat's desire to teach the law and free the land of idol worship. It is believed that Jehoshaphat's son King Jehoram began his short reign of 8 years at the age of 32. King Jehoram was one more king that failed and worshiped idols. Jehoram's alliance with the northern kingdom and his marriage to King Ahab's daughter accomplished little and did not protect him from disease and a painful death. King Uzziah began his reign at the age of 16 and served as king for 52 years. It is believed that King Uzziah was a faithful servant to the one true God and was under the influence of the prophet Zechariah. King Jotham followed the teachings and instructions that were given by the prophets Isaiah, Hosea, Amos, and Micah. He was about 25 years old when he began his reign for 16 years. He inherited a very prosperous kingdom that was built by his father, King Uzziah and received God's blessings. King Jotham feared God and was obedient to God's commands and was careful to listen to the prophets and follow their instructions. The name Azor

CONCLUSION

appears only once in the Bible as part of the genealogy of Jesus within the Gospel of Matthew. The fact that this name only appears once does not in any way minimize the importance of the name Azor. This person was part of God's plan to bring the Savior of the world to this earth. Hezekiah was also responsible for ensuring that Judah would only worship the one true God and purged the temple of all other gods. He was a great and God-fearing king of Judah. However, King Hezekiah made the fatal error in not going to God first before making the decision to begin negotiations with the King of Assyria to avoid complete destruction. King Manasseh was a king that did not follow the godly example of his father Hezekiah. He began his reign at the age of 12 and ruled over Judah for 55 years. King Amon supported the worship of pagan gods and all the other evil practices associated with pagan gods. Unfortunately, he never repented of his evil ways unlike his father, King Manasseh. King Josiah was the youngest recorded king at the age of 8. Josiah grew to be a king that walked with his Lord and kept His commandments and laws. This king wanted to please God; he had all idols removed from the land, and repaired the temple. Josiah was the last King of Judah in the listing before the exile to Babylon recorded by Matthew.

This second listing of Kings in the Messiah bloodline began with Solomon, a great king with many frailties. It is also believed that Solomon wrote the book of Proverbs as a way to share his wisdom in honoring and following God's commands. He also wrote the book Song of Solomon to show the joy of love and marriage from God. However, Solomon's sin was passed to his son Rehoboam who did not listen or seek God's wisdom but listen to the council of those that were in his court. The result was disastrous. Rehoboam lost control of the northern kingdom, Israel, and remained the King for only the southern kingdom of Judah. The second listing of kings is composed of both evil and good kings. Again, we see the worship of idols as a major reason for the destruction of Israel; the exile of their leaders, and the short life for many of the kings in Judah. It is clear God will not tolerate idol worship and those that participate in idol worship will experience God's wrath.

The third listing of the Messiah's ancestors by Matthew includes kings and leaders after King Josiah and ending with Joseph the husband to Mary. The third listing in the Messiah bloodline begins with kings that were exiled to Babylon. It was a common practice for a conquering country to exile the leaders of a defeated country to prevent the leaders from re-establishing themselves at a later date.

King Jechoniah refused to listen to Jeremiah the prophet and he and the people of Jerusalem suffered the consequences. King Jechoniah was king for only a few months before he was captured by the Babylon army and King Nebuchadnezzar. King Jechoniah and those that were related to him and reported to him were all relocated and imprisoned in Babylon for many years while Nebuchadnezzar was in power. King Salathiel like the rest of the royal family during this time period was exiled to Babylon. There is little known about King Salathiel and his activities during this time period. Zerubbabel with the title governor was allowed to lead the Jewish people in returning to Judah and Jerusalem. It was Zerubbabel that lead in the rebuilding of the temple in Jerusalem and the carrying on of the line of David. We know little about the Abiut listed in the Gospel of Mathew. However, God created His church from millions of unknown people over thousands years that worshiped the one true God. The Apostle Matthew listed Eliakim as another unknown name in the bloodline for the Messiah. The name Azor appears only once in the Bible as part of the genealogy of Jesus within the Gospel of Matthew. Sadoc is an unknown name that is only mentioned in the genealogy found in the gospel of Matthew. Achim appears only in Matthew 1 and may be a name that is unique to Joseph's family. The name Eliud is only mentioned once in the Gospel of Matthew as an ancestor of Jesus Christ. Eliud was the great-great-great-grandfather by law of Jesus Christ. It is believed that Eleazar was the father of Matthan and married to Salome. There is little known about Eleazar and his family. The name Matthan is only mentioned once by Matthew in his genealogy found in Matt.1:15. There is little known about Jacob the father of Joseph the husband to Mary. Joseph, Mary's husband was referred to as upright, obedient, protector, and a concerned father.

The third listing by Mathew of the Messiah's ancestors starts with the exile of the Israelites to Babylon and ends with Joseph the husband to Mary and the father of Jesus the Messiah. The time during the exile was a time for the Hebrew people to consider their relationship with their Creator and plans to re-establish themselves as a great nation. Zerubbabel with the title governor was allowed to lead the Jewish people in returning to Judah and Jerusalem. It was Zerubbabel that lead in the rebuilding of the temple in Jerusalem and the carrying on of the line of David. From that point forward within Matthew's listings there is little or no information about those men that carried on the bloodline of the Messiah until Joseph, a mere carpenter. After 400 years of silence, God spoke to Joseph and dispatched His angel,

Conclusion

Gabriel. Joseph and Mary were both descendants of King David and from the tribe of Judah.

Seven hundred years before the birth of Jesus the Messiah, Isaiah prophesied that a virgin shall conceive a son.

Isaiah 7:14 reads, "Therefore the Lord himself shall give you a sign; Behold a virgin shall conceive, and bear a son, and shall call his name Immanuel."

Isaiah 9:6 reads, "For unto us a child is born, unto us a son is given: and the government shall be upon his shoulder: and his name shall be called Wonderful, Counselor, The mighty God, The everlasting Father, The Prince of Peace."

The prophecy that the Messiah would come from the family of David was from God and written by Jeremiah.

Jeremiah 33:15 reads, "In those days, and at that time, will I cause the Branch of righteousness to grow up unto David; and he shall execute judgment and righteousness in the land."

What is striking about the bloodline for the Messiah recorded by Matthew is the fact that it contains both the great patriarchs of faith (e.g. Abraham, Isaac, Jacob) and a number of evil kings. The patriarchs were men of great faith that loved God, listened to his commands, and obeyed Him. It is also believed by some that Matthew intentionally did not record some evil kings. In addition, even some of the great kings (e.g. David, Solomon) were guilty of many sins that in many ways reflected man's fallen condition. God did not exclude evil kings, but included them in the bloodline to make certain that when He became man He took on all the sins of mankind. The bloodline of the Messiah is unique and was controlled by God. Many of the Messiah's ancestors were not selected in the traditional Jewish method of selecting the oldest son. For example, God selected David the youngest of eight sons.

God blessed many of the faithful kings with a long life, great success, and wealth. In many cases those that were involved in sin had their lives cut short and experienced great pain from disease.

Another remarkable aspect of Matthew's genealogy is the fact that he included five women. Jewish tradition at that time would not allow the listing of women in a family genealogy. The women listed were Tamar, Rachab, Ruth, Bathsheba, and Mary. Tamar was a women who was mistreated by her husband and Judah. God is aware of all issues related to injustice for women and will provide the appropriate blessing. Rachab was a harlot who had immense faith in God as she put her life in danger for hiding the spies. This is an excellent example of the importance of not judging someone. Only God knows the heart of people and only God knows those who will make the decision to be a believer. Ruth was a woman who put the well-being of Naomi over her own well-being. It was Ruth's faithfulness that led to her being blessed by God. Bathsheba was a woman who was mistreated by King David and placed in a difficult situation. God blessed Bathsheba and included her in the bloodline to the Messiah. Mary's life was remarkable and divine. Mary was a woman of great faith. Luke 1:38 reads, "And Mary said, Behold the handmaid of the Lord; be it unto me according to thy word. And the angel departed from her." God rewarded Mary's faith and allowed her to give birth to God's only Son, Jesus the Christ the Savior of the world. All of these women and many more were extremely important in unfolding God's plan for all of mankind.

The other unmistakable and often repeated issue that appears throughout the Messiah's bloodline is the worship of idols. This sin was responsible for a great deal of suffering within the bloodline of the Messiah and those living in Judah and Israel. The northern kingdom of Israel was very much involved in worshiping pagan gods and other unspeakable rituals. Those kings that supported these pagan rituals often experienced the wrath of God that resulted in a short life for those Kings. God will not tolerate idol worship and those that participate in idol worship will experience God's wrath, curses and their name will not be remembered. God is a jealous God and will become angry with those who worship idols.

Deuteronomy 29:20 reads, "The Lord will not spare him, but then the anger of the Lord and his jealousy shall smoke against that man, and all the curses that are written in this book shall lie upon him, and the Lord shall blot out his name from under heaven."

God is a jealous God and those that worship other gods will experience His wrath. This is an extremely important command and needs to be taken seriously. Satan is continually attacking the mind and heart of man and is working to convince men to reject the worship of God and worship other idols.

An idol is anything that prevents or separates man from worshiping God. Today, the world worships many different idols. The carved stone statues and mythological gods of the past have been replaced by the worship of money, processions, pleasure and self. Men's mind and heart of today are focused on lusts and dreams of grandeur.

Conclusion

2 Timothy 3:1–2 reads, "This know also, that in the last days perilous times shall come. For men shall be lovers of their own selves, covetous, boasters, proud, blasphemers, disobedient to parents, unthankful, unholy,"

God is the one and only true God of the universe and He revealed himself as Jesus Christ the Savior for all of mankind. Man has turned his back on God and now worships himself and his abilities to solve problems and achieve goals. Idolatry is growing faster today then every before as man refuses to acknowledge God, His love, and His grace.

The worship of money is a world-wide epidemic. Today, man will live out his entire life worshiping money and not realize it is actually an idol. Like man from the time of Christ man today will devote a great deal of time worshiping their money, possessions, and social position. Millions of people throughout this world have devoted their lives to accumulating money and will lie, steal, and kill for more money. Today, both poor and wealthy people worship money and some will spend every waking hour of their lives searching for more money. Millions of people are lost in a fog that has been created by Satan that does not allow man to see his sin and their Savior and Lord.

Matthew 6:24 reads, "No man can serve two masters: for either he will hate the one, and love the other; or else he will hold to the one, and despise the other. Ye canned serve God and mammon."

Idols are very dangerous due to the fact that the worship of idols will provoke God's wrath. The other reason why idols are dangerous is that covetousness is also idolatry. Covetousness is the thoughts and ideas of the mind that are controlled by desires, envy, and greed. Man's fallen nature and his many frailties include desires that are self-centered. Man's Creator God, demands that we are not distracted from our worship of Him with desires of the world. Satan preys on man's weaknesses and has convinced millions that they should live to collect as much wealth as humanly possible. Man's desires also leads to covetousness where man loses control over his craving and begins to covet another man's money and possessions. God demands that man surrenders his entire being to His leading and to make God and His Son his treasure.

1 Thessalonians 1:9–10 reads, "For they themselves show of us what manner of entering in we had unto you, and how ye turned to God from idols to serve the living and true God. And to wait for his Son from heaven, whom he raised from the dead, even Jesus, which delivered us from the wrath to come."

A Christian's greatest love is his love for the one and true God the Creator of the universe. For the Christian the death and resurrection of Jesus Christ has paid the price for his sin and will allow him to escape the wrath of God.

Matthew 22:37 reads, "Jesus said unto him, Thou shalt love the Lord thy God with all thy heart, and with all thy soul, and with all thy mind."

A Christian is not consumed by today's idols or the desire of wealth, but is consumed by God's grace, love, and the desire to obey and worship the God of the universe.

The world today is both passively indifferent or in some cases aggressively opposed to God and the bloodline of His Son the Messiah. The Bible and the Gospel of Christ exposes man's sin and assigns a penalty for committing these sins. The result for rejecting or ignoring God and the gift of His Son is death and spiritual separation from God. Each man needs to surrender and come to that point where he decides to place his life in the hands of his Creator. God's Holy Spirit is waiting to commune with each man to make the decision to place his faith in God's hand. God has made his Holy Spirit available to each man for the purpose of living a life that is pleasing to God. It is only when a man invites God to be the center of his life is he able to fully experience God's blessings.

The world today is engulfed in a spiritual war that is allowing Satan to grow in strength and increase his influence throughout the world.

Matthew 12:43–45 reads, "When the unclean spirit is gone out of a man, he walketh through dry places, seeking rest, and findeth none. Then he saith, I will return into my house from whence I came out: and when he is come, he findeth it empty, swept, and garnished. Then goeth he, and taketh with himself seven other spirits more wicked than himself, and they enter in and dwell there: and the last state of that man is worse than the first. Even so shall it be also unto this wicked generation."

The spiritual condition of the world is deteriorating as more wicked spirits are ever increasing in numbers as they possess more and more men. At no time has the bloodline of the Messiah been more important than now. The worship of idols and the new paganism of today are very dangerous and extremely contagious to all of mankind.

The final covenant made between God and man was not possible without God's bloodline for the Messiah, the Son of David. The bloodline of the Messiah fulfills the prophecy that the Savior of mankind would be born for the purpose of providing forgiveness for all of man's sin with the death of God's Son, Jesus Christ. It provides the scope and depth of God's grace and love for all of mankind.

Matthew 5:17–18 reads, "Think not that I am come to destroy the law, or the prophets: I am not come to destroy, but to fulfill. For verily I say unto you, Till heaven and earth pass, one jot or one tittle shall in no wise pass from the law, till all be fulfilled."

Galatians 3:12–14 reads, "And the law is not of faith: but, the man that doeth them shall live in them. Christ hath redeemed us from the curse of the law, being made a curse for us: for it is written, cursed is every one that hangeth on a tree. That the blessing Abraham might come on the Gentiles through Jesus Christ; that we might receive the promise of the Spirit through faith."

God is the same yesterday, today, and forever. God is the same in both the Old Testament and the New Testament. God gave us both the law of the Old Testament and Jesus of the New Testament. It was God who ended the sacrificial law when He made the final sacrifice of His only Son, Jesus Christ. From that point forward salvation and the forgiveness of sin is made by God's grace through faith.

God's people have always been saved by faith in God. The law defines evil and separates God's people from the evil nations and their evil practices. However, the law clearly shows no human can earn salvation by works or good deeds without faith and God's grace. The birth, life, death, and resurrection of Jesus Christ broke the curse of the law and allowed all of mankind to enter the kingdom of heaven simply by faith.

John 3:16 reads, "For God so loved the world, that he gave his only begotten Son, that whosoever believeth in him should not perish, but have everlasting life."

Ephesians 2:8–9 reads, "For by grace are ye saved through faith; and that not of yourselves: it is the gift of God: Not of works, lest any man should boast."

Today Christians are walking with the Holy Spirit who guides them and requires that they follow God's commandments. When Jesus ascended into heaven He left the Holy Spirit behind to transform people through faith by the grace of God and His son, Jesus Christ.

John 14:26 reads, "But the Comforter, which is the Holy Ghost, whom the Father will send in my name, he shall teach you all things, and bring all things your remembrance, whatsoever I have said unto you."

Jesus told His disciples that when He would leave this world, the Holy Spirit would come to them and would be with them forever. All Christians from that point forward live under God's grace and are taught by the Holy Spirit to love, obey and worship the God of the universe.

The bloodline for the Messiah allowed man access to a number of monumental changes to the status of his existence. Man was given immediate access to the Holy Spirit at the time of his decision to believe in Christ Jesus as his Savior and Lord. The Holy Spirit is actively submitting requests to God on our behalf. The peace of God would permeate the hearts and souls of those who choice to believe. The Spirit of God helps man to understand the will of God in his life. God has given man the magnificent treasure of the Holy Spirit to all who would live a life of faith.

1 Corinthians 2:9-10 reads, "But as it is written, eye hath not seen, nor ear heard, neither have entered into the heart of man, the things which God hath prepared for them that love him. But God hath revealed them unto us by his Spirit: for the Spirit searcheth all things, yea, the deep things of God."

The Bloodline of the Messiah is composed of many generations of both holy and unholy men that were used by God to unfold His plan. The bloodline of the Messiah is extremely important because it fulfills the prophecy of the birth of the Savior and unfolds God's plan for all of mankind.

Bibliography

Spurgeon, Charles H. *Spurgeon's Sermon Notes: Over 250 Sermons including Notes, Commentary and Illustrations,* David Otis Fuller, ed. Grand Rapids, Mt Kregel, 1990.

Buswell, James Oliver Jr. *Problems in the Prayer Life: From a Pastor's Question Box* Chicago: The Bible Institute, 1928.

Geikie, Cunningham. *The life and Words of Christ.* New York: Appleton and Company. 1879.

Brenton, Lancelot C. *The Septuagint with Apocrypha: Greek and English.* Hendrickson, 1986

Bruce, Alexander Balmain, *Training of the Twelve*: Keats Publishing, Inc., 1979

Webster, Douglas D. *Finding Spiritual Direction*: InterVarsity Press, 1991

Lewis, C.S., *Miracles*, Harper One, 2000

Edersheim, Rev. D., *Sketches of Jewish Social Life in the Day of Christ*, Hodder & Stoughton, 1989

Bruner, Frederick Dale, *Matthew A Commentary*, William B. Eerdmans Publishing Company, Cambridge, U.K., 2004

Ryle, J.C., *Holiness*, Renaissance Classics, 2012

www.ingramcontent.com/pod-product-compliance
Lightning Source LLC
Chambersburg PA
CBHW071445150426
43191CB00008B/1240